The Blackout Ripper

The Blackout Ripper

A Serial Killer in London, 1942

Stephen Wynn

PEN & SWORD
TRUE CRIME

An imprint of
Pen & Sword Books Ltd
Yorkshire – Philadelphia

First published in Great Britain in 2022 by
Pen & Sword True Crime
An imprint of
Pen & Sword Books Ltd
Yorkshire - Philadelphia

ISBN 978 1 52671 178 6

A CIP catalogue record for this book is available from the British Library.

Typeset in INDIA By IMPEC eSolutions
Printed and bound in England by CPI (UK) Ltd.

Pen & Sword Books Ltd incorporates the Imprints of Pen & Sword Archaeology, Atlas, Aviation, Battleground, Discovery, Family History, History, Maritime, Military, Naval, Politics, Railways, Select, Transport, True Crime, Fiction, Frontline Books, Leo Cooper, Praetorian Press, Seaforth Publishing, Wharncliffe and White Owl.

For a complete list of Pen & Sword titles please contact

PEN & SWORD BOOKS LIMITED
47 Church Street, Barnsley, South Yorkshire, S70 2AS, England
E-mail: enquiries@pen-and-sword.co.uk
Website: www.pen-and-sword.co.uk

or

PEN AND SWORD BOOKS
1950 Lawrence Rd, Havertown, PA 19083, USA
E-mail: uspen-and-sword@casematepublishers.com
Website: www.penandswordbooks.com

Contents

Introduction

The term "Ripper" originally referred to a tool used to trim the edges of roofing slates. It was then turned in to the somewhat obscene comment "ripping old slates"; the word "slates" being a slang word for prostitutes. It was first used in relation to a serial killer back in the late nineteenth century, when the now infamous "Jack the Ripper" roamed the streets of the Whitechapel area of East London, killing women he believed were prostitutes. It is a topic which has attracted many writers, all of whom have tried to tell the story. But despite this, the true identity of the man who became known as Jack the Ripper has never been conclusively established. There is also a debate to be had over the number of his victims. The accepted total is five, also known as the "canonical five", who were all murdered during a nine-week period between 31 August and 9 November 1888. The women were Mary Ann Nichols, Annie Chapman, Elizabeth Stride, Catherine Eddowes, and Mary Jane Kelly, but a Metropolitan Police file on the case, entitled "The Whitechapel Murders", includes the names of eleven women who were murdered between April 1888 and February 1891.

Whatever the true number of victims Jack the Ripper was responsible for, consideration also has to be given to the fact that the killing of women, especially prostitutes, was not uncommon in Victorian London. Between 1873 and 1899, the cut-up bodies of four women were found in different parts of London, and although the method of murder was different to that of Jack the

Ripper, there were those who claimed it was the work of the same person. There has been much discussion and speculation over the years, but no agreement, as to whether the other six murders were also the work of the same man.

The main reason why Jack the Ripper was credited with murdering only five of these eleven women was because each of their bodies had suffered similar wounds, including deep slash wounds to the throat area, along with extensive mutilations to the abdominal and genital areas, as well as worsening facial mutilations.

Eighty-seven years later, in 1975, another serial killer, Peter Sutcliffe, a lorry driver from Bradford in West Yorkshire, began his killing spree. He would go on to be dubbed by the Press as the "Yorkshire Ripper" and over the next five years would murder thirteen women aged between 16 and 47, a number of whom were prostitutes. He also attacked a further seven women in similar circumstances, all of whom survived. The first of these was an unnamed prostitute, who he attacked in July 1969, six years before he committed his first known murder.

During the investigation, Sutcliffe was interviewed by the police on nine separate occasions, but never charged. On 2 January 1981, he was stopped by police in the Broomhill district of Sheffield, South Yorkshire, and arrested when his vehicle was discovered to be displaying false number plates. Whilst in police custody, he was again interviewed in connection to the Yorkshire Ripper case, as he fitted the description of the killer. The following day police returned to the spot where he had been stopped, only to discover a knife, hammer and rope which had been discarded nearby.

Sutcliffe was also convicted of assaulting a further ten women, as well as being suspected of having committed several other assaults and murders, some of which he later admitted. A number of the women he attacked were known prostitutes. In 1981, when confessing to the attacks and murders, he claimed that the voice of God had sent him on a mission to kill prostitutes.

At the end of his subsequent trial, which lasted for two weeks and finished on 22 May 1981, he was found guilty of all thirteen murders and seven attempted murders. Two of the murders took place in Manchester, with all the others taking place throughout West Yorkshire between 1975 and 1980. He was sentenced to twenty concurrent life sentences and a recommendation that he served a minimum of thirty years before he could be considered for parole, meaning that the earliest he could possibly be freed was May 2011. In July 2010, Sutcliffe was informed that the High Court of Justice in London had decided he should spend the rest of his natural life in prison, what was officially known as a whole life tariff.

There have been three other British serial killers who have also acquired the nickname of "Ripper". In 2000, Alun Kyte, also known as the "Midlands Ripper", was convicted of murdering two women who worked in the sex trade, 20-year-old Samo Paull in 1993, and 30-year-old Tracy Turner in 1994. He was sentenced to life imprisonment with a recommendation that he serve a minimum of twenty-five years.

Anthony John Hardy became known as the "Camden Ripper", having murdered three women, and was also suspected of being responsible for a further five more. In November 2003, he was found guilty of committing the three murders and sentenced to three life terms.

Steven Wright became known as the "Ipswich Ripper" when he murdered five women between 30 October and 10 December 2006. All five women were known prostitutes. In February 2008 he was found guilty on five counts of murder, sentenced to life imprisonment, and given a whole life order. He was also suspected of having attacked and murdered at least four other women.

Yet there is another British serial killer who has been given the title of "Ripper", but is perhaps the least well-known of those already mentioned here. In 1942, during the Second World War, the British public faced the terror of the German Luftwaffe who brought death and destruction to some of the nation's major cities, including its capital, London. But they also faced another terror, a home grown one in the form of Gordon Frederick Cummins, who became known as the "Blackout Ripper" after murdering four women and attempting to murder another two. He was also suspected of the murders of two other women in October 1941, although it was never proved that he was responsible for either of them.

Cummins was somewhat of an enigma. Here was a 28-year-old married man with a doting and attentive wife, who had grown up in a loving and caring family environment and had a good job to return to after the war. He had enlisted in the Royal Air Force (RAF) in 1935 and initially trained up as a "rigger", which meant that he was involved in carrying out flight checks on aircraft before they were cleared for take-off. Liked by his instructors and senior officers, but loathed by many of his fellow servicemen, he proved to be somewhat of a "Walter Mitty" type character; an everyday, ordinary individual who was given to self-aggrandising their dreams or ideas as a way of glamourising an otherwise humdrum life. He lived in a bit of a "twilight" world, where it was almost as if the lies he had been telling for so long had, to him, become his new truth. This all centred around his claims to have been fathered by an unnamed member of the aristocracy, who had been an equerry to King George V, which was of course false. His lies earned him the nickname of "The Count" or "The Duke" from his RAF colleagues, and regardless of what he thought, it was not meant in a nice way.

In 1936, after a short courtship, he married Marjorie Stevens, who worked as a secretary to a West End theatre producer. His relationship with Marjorie appears to have been one of the only close human connections Cummins ever made throughout his adult life.

The "blackout", as it had become termed, had actually begun two days before the outbreak of the Second World War, and was part of the nation's defensive strategy against the threat of German air raids. Despite what it was intended for, the blackout also had the effect of making the streets of London ideal territory for the capital's criminal fraternity. During the years of the war, recorded crime in England and Wales rose by 57 percent, including the serious offences of murder, rape, robbery, burglary and looting.

London, as well as other British cities and large towns, had to ensure that all streetlights were switched off, and that public buildings and private dwellings did not display any light source, which could then be used as a potential guide by German bombers. The British government, via local authorities, ensured that every home throughout the nation was provided with blackout material to cover their windows and doors, each night. It was a boring and laborious task, but one that had to be done in an effort to save lives.

Those who owned a car had the headlights of their vehicles blacked out, which led to many traffic accidents and deaths. Despite not being able to see where they were going, and the speed limit being reduced to just 20 miles per hour during the hours of darkness, some motorists would still drive much too fast for the restrictive conditions in place. The blackout was very strict: even smokers of cigarettes or cigars were forbidden from smoking outdoors during the hours of darkness. Many shops required a second front door in order to prevent light escaping every time a customer entered and left the premises.

At the outbreak of the war, London's civilian population was somewhere in the region of 4.4 million people, and part of the means of helping to keep them safe during the German air raids were shelters, which came in many different forms. Guests at the Dorchester and the Savoy hotels were able to use the buildings' basement shelters, where they could dance and drink the night away. On the other hand, an estimated 1.2 million Londoners had to use Anderson shelters made of corrugated iron that were installed in their back gardens, whilst an estimated 177,000 sought shelter in the comparative safety of the then 79 London underground stations that were available, although a few of these did suffer direct hits during the course of the war, resulting in considerable loss of life.

A number of large, public street-level air raid shelters were built in different locations across London, such as the one in Montagu Place, Marylebone, where Cummins' first victim was discovered, which although maintained as best as they could be in the circumstances, were prone to overcrowding and poor sanitation facilities.

For those who did not want to venture outside to a shelter, the only other option was to stay in one's home and hide in the cupboard under the stairs, or in steel cages known as Morrison shelters.

On 10 July 1940, the Battle of Britain began as the German Luftwaffe launched their quest to defeat the RAF and, in doing so, gain control of the skies above the English Channel and southern England, all in readiness for the expected German invasion of Britain.

On 24 August, and despite Hitler's direct orders not to do so, the city of London was bombed. There is debate surrounding whether or not the raid was accidental or intentional, but one way or another it is likely that this incident was the catalyst for what became known as the Blitz.

Prime Minister Winston Churchill was furious and ordered an immediate attack to be carried out on the German capital, Berlin. The following evening, seventy aircraft from Bomber Command took off from airfields across southern England and made their way across the English Channel and occupied Europe, before dropping their payload on the very epicentre of Nazi Germany. This time it was Hitler's turn to be furious.

From a British perspective, the Battle of Britain ended on 31 October 1940, but this overlapped the start date of the Blitz, which lasted between 7 September 1940 and 11 May 1941.

The Luftwaffe certainly meant business. The first air raid of the Blitz took place over the evening and night of 7 and 8 September 1940, which became known as "Black Saturday", when more than 250 German aircraft dropped a combined weight of 625 tons of high explosive and incendiary bombs across 9 miles of London's Docklands. By the time the raid was over, 436 civilians were dead and another 1,600 had been seriously injured. But the attacks did not stop there. The Luftwaffe, as part of Nazi Germany's attempt to force Winston Churchill to either surrender or enter into peace negotiations, continued these attacks across London, including Buckingham Palace and the West End, for the next fifty-six consecutive nights. In the first month of the Blitz, some 5,730 Londoners were killed and a further 9,000 were injured.

From a German perspective, the Battle of Britain and the bombing of the Blitz was one single campaign, its purpose being to make the British authorities agree to a negotiated peace settlement, although what that would have actually consisted of or looked like, is unclear.

The Battle of Britain resulted in the deaths of 23,002 civilians, with a further 32,138 injured or wounded. In relation to the Blitz, civilian deaths are put between 40,000 and 43,000, with between 46,000 and 139,000 recorded as having been casualties. The Blitz also resulted in the loss or damage of some 2 million homes, with somewhere in the region of 60 percent of these being in London.

German air raids on London continued sporadically all the way through until January 1944, so the threat of air raids for the population of London was a genuine and ever-present threat. People would go to bed at night not knowing if at some point they would have to make a dash for the nearest air raid shelter, or whether their house would still be standing the next morning.

When looking at the above figures, the importance of having a night time blackout become very clear. The problems for the civilian population were compounded, maybe even more so, because for those of the criminal fraternity, the blackout was regarded as a godsend. The darkness provided an advantage and cover for those intending to commit a crime as they were less likely to be seen until it was too late. They were unlikely to be identifiable, and the victim, if still alive, was just as unlikely to be able to provide any kind of description of their assailant. Even today, in the twenty-first century, some local authorities throughout the UK turn off the streetlights in their communities at midnight, meaning anybody out and about on foot after this time is, potentially, in greater danger of being attacked.

Whilst men were away fighting in one of the many different theatres of war, their wives were back home having to fend for themselves, whilst at the same time looking after the family home and doing their bit for the war effort by holding down full-time jobs and managing to stretch out meagre food rations, most of which they would have spent a number of hours standing in queues to obtain.

A number of women, left to their own devices and not knowing if or when they would ever see their husbands again, wanted a bit of glitz, glamour and excitement in their lives. For some of them the only way to earn enough money to live that lifestyle, which was otherwise outside of their day-to-day financial means, was prostitution. It was to London where many of them headed; a city overrun with servicemen looking for a good night out and a bit of female company. There were more than enough men in uniform to go around for the ladies of the night to earn some extra cash, but in January 1942, just before Cummins started his murderous killing spree, 4,000 Americans had made their way across the Atlantic, and whilst on leave, were also out looking to enjoy the bright lights of the city and everything that went with it.

Some women worked full time as prostitutes whilst others were part time. Some worked in brothels, some were street walkers, whilst others worked from a flat. They collectively earned the nickname from American servicemen as the "Piccadilly Commandos". Many of them were controlled by either gangs or pimps.

To the best of our knowledge, three out of the four women who Cummins was charged with murdering were working as prostitutes at the time of their deaths, as was at least one of the girls who he attempted to murder. Of the two additional murders he was suspected of having committed, one of the women, 19-year-old, Maple Churchyard, was, according to the book *Coroner, the Biography of Sir Bentley Purchase,* 'known to have frequently engaged in casual sexual relations with servicemen'.

Incidentally, there appears to be some confusion as to the correct spelling of Maple's name, which is invariably given as either Maple or Mabel. Her surname is also confusingly recorded as either Church or Churchyard, with contemporary newspaper reports giving her name as Maple Church, the England & Wales Civil Registration Death Index listing her as Maple Churchyard, and The National Archives listing her as Mabel Church or Churchyard. For ease of use, however, all further references to her throughout this book will be Maple Churchyard, as that appears to be the one most commonly used.

As Cummins never confessed to murdering any of the women he was accused of killing, it will never be known why he committed these horrific murders. Before his arrest, trial and conviction in 1942, he had no criminal record, nor had he ever shown any history of violence to either men or women. If what linked all these unfortunate women was the fact they were either working as prostitutes, or he believed them to be working as prostitutes, it is pure guess work as to what sparked his need or desire to attack them. The obvious suggestion is that prior to October 1941, by which time he was 27 years of age, Cummins had engaged the services of a prostitute at an unknown time and location, and the experience was such that it somehow triggered his subsequent behaviour.

Chapter One

Family and Early Life

Cummins' story is similar to that of numerous other notorious killers, in so far as if it had not been for the murders and atrocities he committed, he would have passed through life without even a mention in the popular Press. Without the label of "serial killer" wrapped tightly around his neck, he would have been like his peers, just a normal person, doing his bit for King and country during a time of war.

Gordon Frederick Cummins was born in New Earswick, North Yorkshire, on 18 February 1914, to parents John and Amelia Cummins, who had married in York in 1912. His birth was a happy occasion, being a first child for the young couple. His father, John Cummins, who had served as a private in the Royal Army Medical Corps before being medically discharged on 15 March 1919, was in charge of running a school for troubled children. Amelia, meanwhile, was a dutiful wife and mother looking after baby Gordon and the family home.

Macgregor House, the school overseen by John and located at 9 Wine Office Court, Fleet Street, London, first opened its doors in 1886 as a home for working boys aged between 13 and 17, who either had nowhere to live or any family members to look after them. The home provided a roof over their heads, food in their stomachs, and had such amenities as a gymnasium, a library and a reading room to help with their well-being when they were not at work. Accommodation, food and schooling were not free – they had to pay a set weekly fee from the wages they earned – but this was fair and far from being extortionate. In the mid-1890s, a flat rate of 4 shillings and 6 pence was charged, which increased by 2 pence in the shilling for lodging if a boy earned over 6 shillings per week. There were two main rules that the boys had to adhere to: be home by 9.30 pm each evening and attend a place of worship on Sundays.

The establishment was set up and run by a charitable organisation entitled "Homes for Working Boys", and was the brainchild of three friends, Quintin Hogg, Arthur Kinnaird and Ton Pelham. In July 1920, the home moved to 127 Tulse Hill.

The Cummins family must have been relatively well off, as the young Gordon was privately educated at the Llandovery County Intermediate Secondary School. He left in 1930, aged 16, having obtained a diploma in chemistry and continued his studies at the Northampton College of Technology, where he remained until the end of 1932.

During the following two years he worked in different jobs in various parts of the country. On leaving Northampton, he spent time living and working in Newcastle, before returning to Northampton and eventually ending up in London in 1934. His jobs had seen him working as an industrial chemist, a tanner, casual labourer and at a clothing factory, but he clearly had not yet discovered his true path in life.

It is quite clear that he changed somewhat after he moved to London. Maybe it was the bright lights, the hedonism and the allure which exists in nearly all major cities of the world, or the premise that the streets of London were paved with gold that turned his head. Whereas before he appeared to be content with his lot in life, after he arrived in London he no longer found his old way of life attractive. He appeared to want more, hence his claims to be the illegitimate son of a peer, from whom he was provided with an allowance.

The relative family affluence which had provided him with a private education was no longer good enough as far as he was concerned. He had acquired a need for people to think better of him, to believe that he was something he was not. Maybe he had been teased at school because of what his father did for a living, which amongst his peers was perhaps viewed as somewhat of a menial position in comparison to some of the positions their own fathers held.

By day he still worked in a clothing factory where he earned £3 a week, which was about average for the time and when it was normal for a person to have to work a fifty-hour week. But rather than spend his evenings relaxing after a long day's work, he preferred to frequent hotel bars and swanky clubs in the West End of London, often not returning home until the early hours of the morning. In essence he was leading a double life, prompted by what, is unknown, but it was becoming clear that his night-time persona was the one he preferred. Gordon Cummins wanted more out of life, and he was prepared to lie, cheat and steal to get it.

On his soirées to the West End, he certainly did not tell those he found himself in conversation with that he worked in a clothing factory as a leather dresser. Instead, he invented and kept up the pretence that he was the illegitimate son of a peer, who provided him with a generous allowance. His peculiar behaviour became even more bizarre when, in keeping with his claim of coming from regal stock, he insisted on being referred to as "The Honourable" Gordon Cummins.

Possibly because of the political rumblings and uncertainty taking place throughout Europe at the time, on 22 May 1935 the British Government agreed to treble the number of frontline military aircraft in use with the RAF for the defence of the country. This was a massive commitment and meant the production of hundreds more aircraft, pilots, aircrews, mechanics and other members of ground staff. It was at this time that Cummins decided on a career in the RAF, enlisting at the Air Crew Reception Centre at London's Regent's Park, sometime in early 1935.

On 28 December 1936, Cummins married 21-year-old Marjorie Stevens at Paddington Register Office. The couple had first met at the Empire Air Day, which took place at RAF Henlow in May that year. A young and attractive Gordon Cummins, with his enigmatic smile, would have looked resplendent in his smart RAF uniform. A catch for any single and impressionable young woman.

Empire Air Day took place each year at a number of Royal Air Force stations around the country, with usually somewhere in the region of fifty of them taking part. Because of the outbreak of the Second World War, it was a short-lived event, with the first one having taken place on 24 May 1934, and the last being on 20 May 1939.

The idea behind the shows was to allow members of the public to see the Royal Air Force going about their everyday work and commitments, and all monies raised from the events were greatly received by the RAF Benevolent Fund. It was an opportunity for a fun day out, with each station in control of putting on their own shows, albeit with some having similar themes and ideas. The shows themselves included flying displays, the content of which was covered by the King's Regulations and Air Council Instructions, which included the safety precautions that had to be observed at all times, including any flying displays being carried out at a height of 2,000 feet. The year after Cummins and Marjorie Stevens met, the Empire Air Day saw a total of eight fatalities of RAF members at five different stations, who were killed in accidents either during rehearsals or the day of the actual display.

At the time of meeting Marjorie at RAF Henlow in May 1936, Cummins was serving with the Marine Aircraft Experimental Establishment, situated at RAF Felixstowe, in Suffolk. Prior to 1 March 1924, the base had been known as the Marine and Armament Experimental Establishment.

Cummins and his unit remained at Felixstowe until 21 September 1939, by which time it was decided that Felixstowe, due to its location, was potentially vulnerable to enemy air attack, and was moved to Helensburgh, in Dunbartonshire on the west coast of Scotland. Cummins remained stationed at Helensburgh until April 1941, after which he was transferred to the newly opened RAF Colerne in Wiltshire, the construction of which had only begun in 1939. It was during this posting that he was promoted to the rank of leading aircraftman.

His posting in Wiltshire lasted just seven months before he was posted to RAF Falmouth in Cornwall. It was whilst serving in Falmouth that stories first emerge about Cummins not being particularly liked by his colleagues, mainly because of his claims about coming from royal stock, albeit illegitimately. Indeed, he spoke about this aspect of his life so much that he gained the nickname of "The Count" or "The Duke", neither of which were in any way shape or form intended to be complimentary.

At the time of the murders in February 1942, Cummins and his wife, Marjorie, were renting a flat in Southwark, on the south bank of the River Thames in central London. Cummins had been attending a course for initial aircrew training and had been staying at accommodation in Regent's Park, but as it was the weekend, and his course did not begin again until the Monday morning, on Sunday, 8 February he was at home. By this time the couple had been married for just over five years and, rather unusually for the time, especially for a couple who had been married for that number of years, they had no children.

Over dinner Cummins asked his wife if he could borrow £1 (about £45 in today's money), as he was intending to have a night out in the West End. It was a sum of money which she happily and readily handed over. I find this somewhat strange. Here was a young couple who, because of the war and Cummins' commitments in the RAF, could not spend as much time with each other as might be expected of a husband and wife, yet when the opportunity for having a night out presented itself, rather than go out together, Cummins instead chose to go out on his own. It appears that Marjorie did not question this on any level, and furthermore did not seem to have been perturbed about it at all. Nevertheless, there is no suggestion that she had any ideas about her husband's night time exploits, and she certainly would have had no idea about what would take place that week.

Chapter Two

The Victims

The starting point for Gordon Cummins' killing spree was Sunday, 8 February 1942. Something happened inside his head that day which would set in play a string of events that would see him brutally murder four women and attempt to kill a further two. What was it that caused him to behave in such an extreme manner? Unfortunately, Cummins made no statement or admissions, written or verbal, about why he carried out the acts that he was found guilty of, other than to claim that he was not guilty of the offences for which he was charged.

How was it that he managed to be a doting and loving husband to his wife, who at her own admittance stated that he had never once laid a hand on her in anger, yet when away from her he turned in to what can best be described as a "Jekyll and Hyde" character, which allowed him to carry out such depraved and perverse acts of savagery on other women? There are similarities, in that respect, to that of the Yorkshire Ripper, Peter Sutcliffe, who was also a married man at the time he committed his attacks, and whose wife had no idea of his murderous activities.

The majority of Cummins' victims were known to have worked as prostitutes, but it is worth considering what this term meant in the context of the time. During the Second World War, everybody, male or female, was expected to register their name and address with the Ministry of Labour for either war work or to enlist in one of the branches of the British armed forces. This also included prostitutes. Part of the registration form included people having to put down what their occupation was, and although this allowed for job titles as diverse as road sweeper to surgeon, it did not include one for prostitutes. To get round this problem, ministry officials initially included them under Section 174, which was the heading for "Light Entertainment".

In the early years of the war, before the Ministry of Labour decided to place prostitutes under this particular job category, some women intentionally registered as one because word had quickly spread that the Ministry of Labour would not prescribe you a job if an individual had listed their profession as "prostitute". This was because it was highly unlikely any employer would be prepared, or willing, to give them a job.

No branch of the armed services would take them, so the only option was to allocate them for war work. But as soon as a woman who had declared her occupation to be that of a prostitute was sent to a factory, for example, none of the other women would work with or next to them, sit with them in the canteen, or use the same toilets. The women who worked in war-time factories came from all walks of life and from all levels of society. Snobbery was never that far from the surface, as no mother really wanted their daughter to be associating with a known prostitute.

The problem became so widespread as the war went on that the Ministry of Labour decided that when a woman registered with them, if they included "prostitute" on the registration form then they had to produce a receipt from the police to show that they had paid a fine for "living off of the immoral earnings of prostitution", which at the time was usually somewhere in the region of 20 shillings. Without such a receipt, the Ministry would not allow a woman to register her occupation as that of a prostitute.

Evelyn Hamilton

The first of Cummins' victims was 40-year-old Evelyn Margaret Hamilton, who was the manager of a chemist shop in Hornchurch. She was the only one of Cummins' known victims who was not, or had ever been, a prostitute. Her body was found on the morning of Monday, 9 February by a local electrician, Harold Batchelor, who was on his way to work. The body was discovered in an air raid shelter in Montagu Place in Marylebone, West London, which is within a 10-minute walk of Paddington, Hyde Park, Edgware Road, Marylebone and Oxford Street underground stations.

Evelyn Hamilton was born on 8 April 1901 in Heaton, a suburb in the east end of Newcastle-upon-Tyne, to parents Robert James, a colliery labourer, and Mary Emily Hamilton (née Guire). By the time of the 1911 census, Robert and Mary were living at Hall Cottages in Ryton, County Durham, and had been married for eleven years, having wed in 1900 at Newcastle-upon-Tyne.

Evelyn was the eldest of the couple's four children. There were two other daughters; Ethel, who by 1911 was 4 years of age, and baby Kathleen, who was only 4 months old. Their son, John, was 2. Two other children had died either at birth or in their younger years, as the couple had no children at the time of the 1901 census, but ten years later it was recorded that two of their six children had died. Sadly, John would die in 1912, when he was just 4 years of age.

By 1939, according to the General Register Office for England and Wales, Evelyn was living on her own at 6 Elvaston Road,

Ryton, Durham, and her occupation was that of a retail chemist. Coincidentally, one of Cummins' first jobs was in a similar field, when he worked as an industrial chemist.

By all accounts, Evelyn, a charming and intelligent woman, was not the most confident of individuals, especially in social settings; she was quite reserved, had never married, and was not surrounded by a large circle of friends, instead choosing to immerse herself in her work.

What is not known in this case was where or how Cummins and Evelyn Hamilton met on the evening of Sunday, 8 February. Was it in a bar, a hotel, a club, or had he simply accosted her whilst she was walking along the darkened streets of the West End of London? What is known is that Evelyn had left her previous position as the manager of a chemists in what was then rural Hornchurch, and was staying in central London overnight before travelling by train to Grimsby, in Lincolnshire, where she was to take up a similar position.

She arrived in London by rail at Liverpool Street station on the evening in question and caught a taxi from outside Baker Street Underground station, although how she got there is unclear. The distance between the two locations is just over 4 miles, and if she used the Underground, she would have had to take the Central Line to Oxford Circus and change to the Bakerloo Line, or take the Circle Line direct to Baker Street.

At Baker Street, she asked the taxi driver to take her to Gloucester Place, in Bayswater, where it is believed she had booked some accommodation for the night. During the journey she asked if there was somewhere she could get something to eat, and he recommended a restaurant in Oxford Street. After she had dropped her luggage off at her "digs" for the night, she left saying she was going out for a meal. Unfortunately, she never made it to the restaurant, having been murdered within an hour of dropping off her luggage.

Evelyn was last seen alive just before midnight at the Lyons Corner House in Marble Arch drinking a glass of wine. The Corner House was a popular meeting place at the time and was the starting point for many a night out in the West End. Its popularity was due to the fact that it was possible to obtain food and drink there 24 hours a day, thus making it a regular haunt for servicemen enjoying a night out in London.

It has been (wrongly) suggested that Evelyn was out celebrating her 41st birthday. This is clearly incorrect, however, as her birthday was on 8 April and at the time of her death, she was just two months shy of her 42nd birthday.

Divisional Detective Inspector Clare of Scotland Yard, the lead detective in the case, initially concentrated his enquiries on Evelyn's movements between the time of her arrival at Liverpool Street station and when she arrived at Baker Street, knowing that her knowledge of London was limited.

However, it is highly unlikely that Evelyn was simply out late at night walking round the streets of Marylebone for a breath of fresh air. The other element of her death which is unclear was whether Cummins attacked her somewhere near the shelter where she was found and simply disposed of her body by dumping it in there, or whether he dragged her inside the shelter before killing her.

There is a strong possibility that Cummins was also in the Lyons Corner House at the same time as Evelyn Hamilton. It is possible that he spotted her in there, noticed she was on her own, waited until she left and then followed her. This is the only scenario that makes sense as to how the two of them were in the same place at the same time. Evelyn was not a prostitute, and it could even be said that she was socially inept, thus making it unlikely that she was confident enough to have started or engaged in conversation with a total stranger, even a handsome looking one in military uniform.

Her death is different from the murders of the other three women in so far as there is no evidence to suggest that she had been sexually assaulted. Nor had her throat been cut or her body mutilated. Although fully clothed, her skirt had been pulled up around her waist, her underwear pulled down and her blouse was torn to such a degree that one of her breasts was visible. However, this could just as easily have been the result of her struggle to fend her attacker off, rather than by any attempt by him to remove her clothing. A scarf she had been wearing, and which had clearly been used to strangle her, was still wrapped tightly around her neck when her body was discovered.

Evelyn's handbag, which besides other items contained £80 in cash, was found to the north of Montagu Place in nearby Wyndham Street, which sits in between Knox Street and Enford Street. The amount of money, around £3,600 in today's figures, was a staggering amount for somebody to have been carrying around with them at that time. Why would a woman be walking around London in the early hours of the morning with such a large sum of money in her handbag?

Another puzzle was why a number of personal items belonging to Evelyn, such as a comb and purse, and which had clearly been in her handbag previously, were found on the ground immediately outside of the air raid shelter. It was as if they had been emptied out of the bag, yet her handbag, as we know, was found some streets away. If her attacker had taken it when he fled the scene, why empty it and then take it with him, and in doing so risk having to answer some potentially awkward questions if he was subsequently seen and stopped by a policeman? There is, of course, the possibility that even if her attacker had taken the handbag away from the actual scene of the crime, he could have dropped it a short while later, before it was found and picked up by someone else who then dropped it in Wyndham Street, where it was finally found by a patrolling policeman. All Evelyn's personal belongings that were found in and around the air raid shelter were gathered up by the police and examined. Unfortunately, no fingerprints were recovered from any of the items.

From the strangulation marks found around her throat, Home Office pathologist Sir Bernard Spilsbury was able to establish that she had been attacked and strangled by a left-handed man, but there were no definitive leads to establish who had been responsible for committing such a heinous crime. Evelyn's body had sustained a number of cuts and scratches, but these were commensurate with the struggle which she had clearly put up whilst being attacked. There would most likely have been a time during the attack when she would have realised that it was not just an assault or an attempt to rape her, but that whoever it was intended to kill her, and she was literarily fighting for her life.

There is no suggestion that on the night of her murder Evelyn Hamilton was, or had ever been, working as a prostitute. Sadly for her she was simply in the wrong place at the wrong time, and her attacker, who had presumably been out in the same area drinking for most of the evening, was overcome by his desire and need to sate the murderous urges he was visited by before he returned to his lodgings for the night.

It was thanks to the efforts of Sir Bernard Spilsbury that the murders committed by Gordon Cummins were investigated in such detail. By the time of the "Blackout Murders", Spilsbury's reputation as a forensic pathologist was extremely high. Back in April 1924, he was involved in the investigation of the murder of 38-year-old Emily Kaye, who had been killed by her lover, 34-year-old Patrick Mahon, at a rented property known as the "Officers House" in Eastbourne, East Sussex. The murder of Emily Kaye was a particularly gruesome one, as after her death Mahon dismembered her body, burning some of the remains whilst boiling other parts.

Spilsbury was asked to go to the crime scene to help locate some of Kaye's missing body parts in order to determine what parts still needed to be found. On arriving at the Officers House, Spilsbury was aghast to witness a detective picking up pieces of Kaye's dismembered body with his bare hands, before placing them in an unsterilized bucket. Shocked that a supposedly experienced police officer could be dealing so carelessly with what would ultimately be evidence in the prosecution's case, he asked the man why he was not wearing a pair of rubber gloves? The man replied that he had never worn gloves, nor had he ever heard or seen any of his colleagues wearing gloves since the Metropolitan Police Service's murder squad had been formed back in 1907. Spilsbury was so flabbergasted by the man's reply that after he had finished at the crime scene, he returned to London and sought out Detective Superintendent William Brown, the head of the Metropolitan Police's murder squad, to tell him about the conversation he had had with one of detectives. Out of this was born what became referred to as the "Murder Bag"; literarily a bag that any detective who was dispatched to a perspective murder scene would take with them to ensure that the best possible evidence could be collected, whilst at the same time reducing the risk of that same evidence from being contaminated.

There was no real mystery about the contents of the Murder Bag. Initially it contained a pair of rubber gloves, a magnifying glass, a ruler, what we would know today as cotton buds, a pair of tweezers, evidence bags and a compass.

The forensic evidence which in part helped convict Cummins, only came about because of Spilsbury's attention to detail and what he had seen in 1924, during the murder case of Emily Kaye.

Evelyn Oatley (AKA Leta Ward)

Evelyn Judd was born on 5 April 1909 in Earby, a small village on the borders of Lancashire and Yorkshire that was historically part of the West Riding of Yorkshire. By the time of the 1911 census, Evelyn and her elder brother, Herman, were both living with John and Catherine Sierman and their 21-year-old son, also John, at 20 Leeds Street, Keighley, Yorkshire. There was no reference to either of her parents.

For a youngster growing up in such a small and close-knit community at the turn of the twentieth century, they would have been as far away from the bright lights of a big city as it was possible to be.

On 25 June 1936, Evelyn Judd became Mrs Evelyn Oatley when she married Harold Oatley, a hard-working and kindly individual. They had originally met in Blackpool in 1932, at a time when she worked as a chorus line girl at the Windmill Theatre in Great Windmill Street, London. The theatre was famous for having naked women on stage and was based on the Paris cabaret music halls such as the Folies Bergère and the Moulin Rouge.

Being one of the famous naked "Windmill Girls" would have brought Evelyn to the attention of many men, most of whom would have been older and wealthy individuals, which would have no doubt brought her many offers, both moral and immoral ones, from those who were infatuated by her beauty.

Before the arrival of the Windmill Girls, who appeared on stage in motionless poses like living statues, being able to view a naked woman in a theatre production had been prohibited by the laws surrounding obscenity and morality. This was surpassed when the official censor had to agree that nude statues could not be classed as morally objectionable.

Evelyn's new husband, Harold Oatley, a retired chicken farmer, provided her with the love, affection and stability she had sought most of her life. In general, English society in the early 1930s was still one based on morals and standards, which included the expectation that a woman should be a virgin on her wedding night. At a time when a wife was seen through the eyes of society as the "property" of her husband, there were not many men who wanted, or would even consider taking, a woman as his wife who was not virginal. But it appears Harold was not a man to be put off by such matters. Shortly after Evelyn and Harold had met, she told him that not only was she not a virgin, but some years earlier she had given birth to a child who had been given up for adoption.

Despite being married to a loving and considerate husband, Evelyn had started to find the solitude and comparative isolation of living in the country boring and unattractive, and the lure of city life and the bright lights of London started to call her once again. After a year of married life Evelyn returned to live in London, and although her days of being one of the Windmill Girls were over (having been replaced by younger and prettier girls), she was still greatly attracted to the city nightlife and all that it had to offer. Nights out drinking, dancing and being in the company of attractive, well-dressed and confident young men was what she craved the most.

Although Evelyn and Harold lived separate lives, with her in London and Harold still at the matrimonial home in Blackpool, they remained together and on friendly terms, caring for each other in their own individual ways. Indeed, Harold had even been down to stay with Evelyn the month prior to her death.

In London Evelyn earnt a living as a nightclub hostess, obtaining work wherever and whenever she could find it. Work in the night-time economy was, by its very nature, flexible. To supplement the money she earned as a hostess, Evelyn, using the name of Leta Ward, became a prostitute. With the outbreak of the Second World War, clients, especially those in the military, were plentiful, as people looked to enjoy themselves the best that they could, not knowing when the fragility of everyday life would finally catch up with them.

Late on the evening of Monday, 9 February 1942, Evelyn was out in the West End looking to earn some extra money when she met a man outside a restaurant in Shaftesbury Avenue, in the very heart of the city's theatre land. Witnesses would later describe the person she met as being a moustachioed man wearing an RAF uniform, about 5 feet 8 inches tall with short brown hair.

Evelyn was last seen alive just after 11.30 pm that same evening, when her neighbour, Ivy Poole, who also lived in one of the flats which made up 153 Wardour Street, saw her arrive at the property with a man wearing an RAF uniform, and who she would later describe in exactly the same way as the three witnesses who had seen the couple outside the restaurant in Shaftesbury Avenue.

It would seem Ivy Poole was unconcerned about seeing Evelyn coming home with a man, and there was every likelihood that she knew what her neighbour did for a living.

By midnight, Ivy Poole was already asleep in her bed because not long after, she was awoken by music coming from the radio in Evelyn's room, which had suddenly become louder. Other than being woken from her sleep, Ivy did not really give the increase in the volume of music much thought and quickly went back to sleep.

At about 8.30 am on Tuesday, 10 February, Evelyn's partly clothed and mutilated body was discovered on her bed by two men who had come to read the meter in her room. The sight that greeted them was a gruesome one to say the least. She had heavy bruising to her face and chest and had been strangled, but only enough to render her unconscious. Her death was the result of the severing of the carotid artery in her neck. In essence, she had bled to death. However, it was what her attacker did to her body after he had killed her that was the real shock and horror story. Using a razor blade, a piece of broken mirrored glass from a compact in her handbag, and an old fashioned, hand-held tin opener that he had taken from the cutlery draw in the kitchen, he had mutilated the area of her stomach, genitals and upper thighs. Most of the wounds had been inflicted in the immediate area of her vagina using the tin opener. Evelyn had also been sexually assaulted with a torch, which was discovered sticking out of her vagina. A pair of curling tongs owned by Evelyn, which had also been used by her attacker to assault her with, were found on the bed near to her body. The contents of her handbag had been strewn across the floor of her room, as if the killer had been urgently looking for something, although what this might have been is unclear.

The attacker must have managed to overcome Evelyn relatively quickly as her body had no defensive wounds, and no skin or hair particles were recovered from underneath her nails, as might be expected if a victim had been in a position to defend themselves from their assailant.

The police recovered fingerprints from the piece of broken mirrored glass that was found in Evelyn's handbag, as well as from the tin opener, but they did not find a match in their fingerprint records system. The subsequent value of the fingerprints the police recovered from some of the crime scenes associated with the murdered women was largely down to the work of Scotland Yard's Detective Chief Superintendent Frederick Cherrill, who was one of the world's foremost fingerprint experts of the day, as well as being somewhat of a hand writing expert. Indeed, as a Detective Superintendent, Cherrill was awarded an MBE by King George VI in July 1943 for his work in the advancement of fingerprint identification, which included the investigation of the Cummins case. In response to a question from a reporter from the *Daily Mirror* newspaper, asking whether Cherrill had taken the King's fingerprints, he responded by saying, 'Well, I wouldn't be at all surprised if I hadn't got them here'. After which he gently tapped his jacket pocket where he had placed the case containing his MBE.

By the time of his retirement from the Metropolitan Police service in 1953, Cherrill's department at Scotland Yard had amassed a collection of more than 1 million fingerprints of suspects and convicted individuals. In July 1954, he published a book entitled *Cherrill of the Yard*, which detailed his forty years' service as a police officer, but in particular focused on the many famous cases he had been involved in that heavily featured fingerprint evidence, which, of course, included that of Cummins.

Margaret Florence Lowe (AKA Peggy Campbell)

Although born in the city of Napier, on New Zealand's North Island, prior to living in London Margaret Lowe had been a resident of Southend-on-Sea, Essex, with her husband, Frederick and their daughter Barbara, and had helped to run the family's fancy goods business selling small decorative items and knick-knacks.

The 1911 census shows 29-year-old Frederick Lowe and his wife, Alice, whom he had married in 1910, living at 71 Surbiton Road, Southchurch, Southend-On-Sea. Alice, who had worked with Frederick as an assistant in his fancy goods shop, died on 18 August 1918 at the age of 37. In her will she left Frederick the relatively substantial sum of £564 9s 7d (£32,000). The following year, possibly because of his newfound wealth, Frederick joined the Freemason's when he became a member of the Albert Lucking Lodge in Southend.

In 1919, when she was 20 years of age, Margaret was working as a prostitute in London, but just two years later, on 11 October 1921, she married widower Frederick Lowe in Rochford, Essex, and worked with him in his shop at 19 Pier Approach, Southend-On-Sea. How or where the couple had met is unclear.

Life was pleasant for Margaret until Frederick died suddenly and unexpectedly on 14 December 1932, aged 51. There then appear to be two different versions of what happened to Margaret Lowe, and where life took her.

According to one theory, sometime in 1934 Margaret made what appears to have been a rather strange decision. She placed her daughter Barbara, who was roughly 7 years of age, in a boarding school and moved to London where she initially found work as a domestic cleaner. It was not a job she did for long, and whether she found no enjoyment in the work, or the relatively poor pay was insufficient for her needs, she took the drastic decision to change her career path and once again earn her living as a prostitute. It was something she was quite comfortable with and had no hang ups about. Maybe she did it to help pay for her daughter's education, after all, boarding school fees would not have been cheap.

According to another theory by Michael J. Buchanan-Dunne (murdermiletours.com), after Frederick died Margaret became enveloped with depression and found solace in consuming large quantities of alcohol. The family run business was no more, her home was boarded up and her daughter Barbara was taken into care.

Whatever the correct story was concerning her daughter, Margaret had by no means cut off all ties with her. She saw Barbara on average every three weeks when she travelled down to Southend to spend the weekend with her. They would take picnics, go to the pictures, and spend time walking along the seafront and the town's pier. Margaret did her very best to make those weekends as pleasant and memorable as she possibly could.

By February 1942, Margaret herself was no longer the stunningly attractive woman she had been in her younger years. Nevertheless, she was always elegantly dressed and smartly turned out. In the winter months she wore a fur coat to shield herself against the bitter cold as she made her way around the West End looking for potential customers. This also had the added bonus of making her appear to have a certain air of sophistication.

Like Evelyn Oatley, 43-year-old Margaret Lowe had been working as a prostitute at the time of her death. She had left her flat at 11 Gosfield Street, Marylebone, on the evening of Tuesday, 10 February and had gone looking for customers. At just after 1 am the following morning she was seen by a neighbour, Florence

Bartolini, returning to her flat with a man. Sometime later Bartolini heard Margaret's front door being closed and the sound of what she took to be a man whistling. Bartolini assumed, somewhat understandably, that Margaret and her client had completed their transaction and the man had simply left. Little did Bartolini know about what had taken place inside Margaret's flat.

Margaret's daughter, Barbara, who was only 15 years of age at the time, was the person who made the horrific discovery of her mother's body two days later, having travelled to London from Southend to stay with her for the weekend. Making such a discovery would have been a traumatic experience for anybody, but the feelings of shock and horror that a 15-year-old girl would experience when discovering the body of her murdered mother can only be guessed at.

Margaret was laying on her back in bed. The covers had been pulled up to her chin and it was abundantly clear that her body had been carefully placed in a particular position after she had died, rather than having been left on the bed as it was when she was killed.

An examination of her body by forensic pathologist Sir Bernard Spilsbury revealed that she had been badly beaten and that the cause of death had been strangulation via a silk stocking, which was still pulled tightly around her neck. It would have been clear and obvious to even the most untrained eye that Margaret had been badly beaten. In his autopsy report Sir Bernard commented that the injuries which had been inflicted on her body were, 'quite dreadful' and that the person responsible was 'a savage sexual maniac'.

It was clear that her attacker had gone into a sexual frenzy when he had killed Margaret. Not satisfied with using just one implement to kill her, he had picked up numerous items including a poker, a razor blade, a table knife, a vegetable knife, and a serrated bread knife. Her abdomen had been cut open exposing a number of her internal organs, and the similarities to the murders of the infamous Jack the Ripper in the East End of London in the late 1880s could not be ignored. Each of the Ripper's victims had had their throats slit, their stomachs opened up, and were stabbed numerous times in their abdomen and genitals. When the autopsy was conducted on Margaret Lowe, a candle was still protruding from her vagina, a bread knife was still embedded in her groin and there were numerous cuts and slash marks all over her body.

Like the crime scene at the murder of Evelyn Oatley, a number of fingerprints were recovered from objects found in Margaret's flat, including a candlestick holder, a drinking glass, and a partially drunk bottle of stout. The prints were sufficiently sharp enough to establish that they were from a person's right hand.

It must be said that the injuries inflicted on Evelyn Oatley were appalling by anyone's standards, but those inflicted on Margaret Lowe surpassed even those levels of savagery. It was clear that the killer had been in no rush to conclude his acts of brutality, knowing full well that being in the sanctity of Margaret's flat, he was unlikely to be interrupted.

Sir Bernard Spilsbury, the forensic pathologist who conducted the autopsy on Margaret Lowe, had also carried out the autopsy on the body of Evelyn Oatley. Taking in to account the location of the murder scene, the time scale and the injuries inflicted, it would have been clear to Sir Bernard that the same man had been responsible for both murders. The obvious concern was how quickly the ferocity of the attacks had intensified, with the real worry being about what the murderer would potentially do to their next victim. The race was on to find the murderer before he could kill again.

Catherine Mulcahy (AKA Kathleen King)

Little is known of the life of Catherine Mulcahy prior to her being attacked, but on Thursday, 12 February1942 she was 25 years of age and a known prostitute, who also used the working name of Kathleen King. She met the man who would later attack her after he had managed to slip out from his accommodation block. He was a handsome man who looked smart in his RAF uniform, and she was happy to take him back to her flat at Southwick Street, Paddington, which was close to both Paddington station and Hyde Park.

It was particularly cold that evening, so cold in fact that it had snowed, making the idea of walking any great distance out of the question for most people who were on a night out in the West End, and with time being of the essence for both of them, a taxi was a better option than a journey on the Underground.

The agreed fee for the interaction between them was £2 (approximately £90), a sum which was handed over before they had even managed to flag down a cab. On arriving at her flat the taxi driver was paid and the pair went inside. Without any further ado they went straight to the bedroom, where she began seductively removing her clothes while he watched. Whilst undressing, she left her boots on because the floor was cold, and she had only lit her gas fire when she had returned home so it took a while for the flat to be sufficiently warm enough for her to feel comfortable whilst undressing. The decision to leave her boots on would prove to be one that would ultimately save her life.

Once she was fully undressed, she smiled and invited the man
to join her on the bed, a routine she had gone through numerous
times before. He then quickly removed his own clothes in an
expectant fashion and sat astride her. But sex was the last thing
on his mind. What he wanted to do was not going to be enjoyable
for Catherine by any stretch of the imagination. His only intention
was to strangle, kill and no doubt mutilate her body, a desire he
had had from the moment they had first met, and which had been
the reason for his night out in the first place.

Thankfully, however, things did not quite go according to plan.
Her attacker quickly moved position and jabbed his knees into
Catherine's stomach, grabbing her by the throat with both hands as
he did so. Pinned to the bed and in an extremely precarious situation,
Catherine must have instinctively known that if she simply lay on
the bed submissively, without trying to defend herself, she would
soon be dead. Instead, she began struggling and somehow managed
to manoeuvre her legs up and underneath the man's body, before
kicking him in the stomach with her booted feet. A combination of
brute strength and a strong desire to stay alive saw her find an inner
strength which she did not even know she possessed.

The kick she landed was sufficiently painful enough to force
her attacker to remove his grip from around her throat. Catherine
continued to struggle with all the strength she could muster,
which resulted in the man falling from the bed and landing on
the floor. Grabbing her opportunity, Catherine ran naked and
screaming from her flat to one of her neighbours. Realising he
could find himself in an extremely difficult situation, her attacker
threw a £5 note on the bed, hoping this would be sufficient to
buy her silence. Perhaps he thought to himself that because his

intended victim was a prostitute, why would someone who plied such a trade want to go to the police, and even if she did, would they even believe her?

Quickly dressing himself as best he could in the circumstances, with his tunic and shirt only partly buttoned up, he looked every bit like a man in a rush. On his way out he walked past an extremely agitated Catherine, who was stood in the doorway of her neighbour's flat. He pulled a wad of bank notes from his trouser pocket before handing her a further £8 and saying, 'I'm sorry, I think I've had too much to drink this evening,' before grabbing his greatcoat and leaving. He was in such a hurry that he did not realise he had left behind his RAF webbing belt, which would eventually prove to be excellent evidence when it came to convicting Cummins of his crimes.

It was not uncommon for prostitutes to receive short shrift from the police when it came to reporting physical attacks. In some cases, women simply did not want the police to know how they earned their living, but despite such concerns, Catherine decided to report the matter to the police.

Somewhat amazingly, despite the close call the attacker had had with Catherine Mulcahy, he was not deterred sufficiently enough to appreciate his good fortune and return to his billet as fast as his feet could carry him. Instead, he remained in the West End and actively went looking for another victim, and it would not take long for him to find one.

Doris Jouannet (AKA Doris Robson/Olga)

Doris Elizabeth Robson was born in Northumberland on 21 March 1909. Being born out of wedlock and with her mother dying not too long after her birth, she did not exactly have the best start in life. Why she moved to London and turned to prostitution is unknown, but logic suggests the bright lights of the big city and the lure of a better life was what drew her to the capital. She was clearly there by 1935 as on 4 November that year, she married Frenchman Henri Jouannet at Paddington Registry Office, by which time he was 60 years of age, thirty-four years older than Doris.

It is likely they met through her work as a prostitute when he became one of her regular clients. Henri soon became infatuated with this pretty, younger woman, and he was in a position to be able to look after her financially and provide her with the lifestyle she had craved, and marriage was simply part of the deal, along with her agreement to quit her previous way of life.

Henri Jouannet was everything that Doris was looking for in a man, at least in a material sense. He had a good job as the manager of the Royal Court Hotel in Sloane Square, a home, plenty of money, he was kind and treated her nicely. He could even afford to be driven round in a chauffeur-driven Rolls Royce motor vehicle.

The 1939 England and Wales Register shows Henri and Doris Jouannet living at 33 Enys Road, Eastbourne, in a town house which consisted of five flats. By the early weeks of 1941, less than a couple of weeks before Doris was murdered, the couple had moved into their new home in Sussex Gardens, West London. What led directly to Doris's death was not the move to London, but her inability to give up her life as a prostitute. Maybe it was the excitement and thrill of doing something she knew she should not be doing. Maybe it was being desired by younger, more attractive and fitter men that drew her back to her old ways; an aspect of life that Henri was simply not able to provide for her.

Before the war Henri and Doris had enjoyed as good a standard of living as was possible for most people to have. They could afford to eat and drink in the best restaurants, and Doris wore some of the finest clothes money could buy. They even had servants to look after them. Once the war started, however, hotels were affected massively. Staying at a hotel, especially four- and five-star ones was not that high on the list of things people wanted to do. Tourism became nearly non-existent. The usual form of travel from far off destinations such as America, Australia, South Africa and India was by ship, and with German submarines travelling throughout the world's major waterways, any vessel heading towards the United Kingdom was, as far as Germany saw it, a legitimate target. London found itself being bombed on an almost daily basis by the German Luftwaffe throughout the time of the Blitz. With this in mind, the hotels such as the one Henri managed were simply not getting as many customers coming through their doors. Business not only plummeted, it came almost to a grinding halt. For Henri and Doris, money was suddenly not so plentiful, but Doris had become accustomed to a certain standard of living, one that she liked and was unprepared to give up.

With Henri having to spend much of his time working nights, Doris had the opportunity to once again ply her trade as a prostitute to earn herself some extra money on top of the ever-shrinking weekly allowance that Henri provided her with. But for her there would be no walking the streets and fighting with the "other girls" for the attention of drunken servicemen who wanted a "quicky" down some dark, dingy alleyway. She was above that. Here was an attractive woman for her age, who at over 6 feet in her high-heels, was always immaculately dressed, slim, with an air of sophistication about her: traits a number of well-to-do clients found both attractive and appealing.

Doris sometimes used her maiden name of Robson and was also known simply by the slightly more exotic name of Olga, which, said with the subtle hint of a foreign accent, made her extremely desirable to perspective clients. It is uncertain if Henri was aware of his wife's night-time soirées into the West End, but it is extremely unlikely that he was.

Maybe working as a prostitute was not just about the money. It was possible that she missed the life which she once had. She could have been bored and simply wanted some excitement in her life, or maybe it was because she enjoyed being desired and wanted by other men. Whatever the reason, the extra money she earned from having sex with other men would definitely come in handy. What is curious is how she managed to hide all of her nefarious earnings from Henri, who must have known that she was spending more money than he was providing for her.

Regardless of what the primary reason was behind her return to prostitution, it still draws a picture of a somewhat dis-functional if not unhappy marriage. This may have been due to the age gap between them, but it might also have been because the hotel industry, especially in London, had been greatly affected by the war which had seen a massive decline in the number of guests staying in hotels, making it a very stressful time for Henri. Maybe their marital problems were down to nothing more sinister than Henri simply not paying his younger wife enough attention.

On the evening of Thursday, 12 February, the same evening which saw Catherine Mulcahy attacked in her flat in Paddington, Doris Jouannet escorted her husband to the tube station for him to return to work for the night. However, Doris did not immediately go back home, because with Henri back at work and out of the way, she had no intention of having a quiet night in. For her the plan was to meet as many clients as she could, with her main aim being to earn as much money as possible. Sometime whilst out and about in the West End on that cold and wet evening, Doris met the man who would become her brutal and sadistic killer.

She had initially met a friend, Beatrice Lang, and had a drink with her in a nearby tearoom. As usual, she was immaculately dressed: being stylish and fashionable was important to Doris. On leaving the tearoom the two women made their way to Oxford Street where they parted company. Beatrice would later recall that they went their separate ways at around 10.20 pm, when she was going back home to her cosy flat, whilst Doris was going to meet one of her regular clients. However, Beatrice did not know where he lived, and it was an appointment she never kept.

Soon after having said goodbye to Beatrice, and before she arrived at her client's home, Doris met her attacker. Where, or how they met is not known, but whether it was because he offered her more money than her regular client, or because she fell for his charm and good looks, she took his money and let him in to her ground floor flat at 187 Sussex Gardens, in fashionable and prestigious Bayswater. It is even possible the two had met previously and the man knew where she lived and simply took the chance of calling at her home to see if she was working.

Doris removed most of her clothing in preparation for having sex, which would have presumably been paid for soon after they had met. If his mindset was the same as it had been with the other women he had murdered, sex would have been the last thing on the man's mind. If his previous actions were anything to go by, he would have struck quite early on in the proceedings, taking

Doris completely by surprise. The most she would have been considering, however, was whether he be rough or considerate in his love making.

What followed would have been absolutely horrendous for Doris. The fear, suffering and pain she must have experienced can only be guessed at, and it was most definitely not the end she deserved. Right up to the moment that her attacker struck, changing from being a paying customer into an alcohol fuelled, murdering psychopath, it would have been a routine that Doris had calmly gone through hundreds of times before, never once thinking that her life was in danger.

When Henri Jouannet returned home from work the following evening to have dinner with Doris, as was his routine when he was working nights, he placed the key in the front door of his flat, unlocked it and stepped inside. He called out to Doris, but there was no reply, which was unusual to say the least. However, he was more surprised than he was concerned or worried. Maybe she was out shopping or had gone to visit a neighbour? He then he discovered that not only was their bedroom door shut, it was locked as well. He was not a physically weak individual, but at 67 years of age, neither was he strong enough to break down the bedroom door. If his wife was inside, why had she locked the door and why was she not responding to his calls? There was nothing he could find or think of that he could use to force the door. His pulse and heartbeat began to race as his initial feeling of uncertainty was replaced by panic and concern.

Henri called upon one of his neighbours to enquire if they had seen or heard anything of Doris, but they had not. This was not the response he wanted to hear, as all it did was to fuel his feeling of dread and woe.

During the Second World War there were few families who were sufficiently wealthy enough to be able to afford a telephone in their home. Most working-class people did not have a wide enough circle of friends who were "on the phone", so for most there was little or no need to possess such a luxury. Most businesses, companies, organisations, shops, restaurants, and the police had telephones, and for the general population there were public payphones situated throughout the community.

Fortunately for Henri, one of his neighbours had a telephone installed in their flat, which they happily allowed him to use to call the police. The news for the assistance of a constable was received at Paddington Police Station, which was only about 1 mile away from where Henri and Doris lived. In the war-torn London of 1942, most policing duties were carried out on foot, and it was constable William Payne who was quickly dispatched to assist Henri with his "problem".

On his arrival at the Jouannets' home, Constable Payne spoke with a by now heavily distraught Henri, who had begun to fear the worst. The bedroom had a window, but after quickly assessing the situation and giving the matter some consideration, Constable Payne quickly established his best option was to use brute force against the bedroom door. He made his intentions clear to Henri as to what he wanted him to do, and with a nod of the head from Henri, Payne lined himself square on to the door. Taking one step backwards before propelling himself forward as fast as he could, his size nine boot made contact with the door immediately adjacent to the lock. The door frame partly shattered with a loud cracking noise, and although Payne's kick was not quite enough to force the door entirely open, it had still done enough damage for him to forcefully shove it open with his shoulder.

Other than the fine glow emanating from a small electric fire, the room was in darkness. Before entering the room, in a firm but considerate tone of voice Constable Payne requested Henri take himself out into the hallway. Payne entered the room and reached round to the wall to his right and switched on the light. Sprawled across the bed, just a couple of feet in front of him, was the body of a woman lying diagonally from corner to corner, naked in part except for a black night gown, which adorned her body whilst displaying her female charms in equal amounts.

Although shocked at what he had discovered, Payne took a deep breath, composed himself, and managed to stay calm and professional as he knew he had to. Regardless of what he was feeling on the inside, it was vital he did not panic or appear flustered.

As he left the bedroom, he pulled the door closed behind him as best he could, telling Henri that under no circumstances was he to attempt to enter the room. He then went to the neighbour's flat with the telephone, asking the occupant for some privacy whilst he made his call to the police station.

The phone call started a flurry of visits to the Jouannet's flat. First to arrive was Detective Inspector Leonard Clare, who was also the first person to examine what was now officially a murder scene. After a brief conversation with Constable Payne to ascertain the facts, he entered the bedroom. It was clear to him that Doris Jouannet was dead, of that there was absolutely no question, but what he wanted to do was to try to establish how she had met her end. The first thing he noticed was a stocking which had been tied and knotted tightly round her neck. On closer examination, however, he could see that her jaw was broken, suggesting that she had been struck forcibly in the face before being strangled with the stocking. The blow to her face, which may well have been a punch due to the fact there was no open wound, had perhaps stunned or even knocked her unconscious before she was strangled, as she otherwise appeared to have no obvious defensive wounds to her hands.

As his gaze turned to her body, Clare would have no doubt needed a moment to compose himself as he took in the scene before him and was fully able to comprehend the true horror of the brutality which had been inflicted upon Doris Jouannet's body.

Her torso had been extensively mutilated with slashes, stab wounds and cuts to her abdomen, vaginal area, the underneath of her left breast, and both of her thighs. Scribbling down notes as he went, Clare could not help but draw attention to three of the wounds. There was a particular nasty wound to her vagina, and another which he estimated to be a 6-inch wound that ran between her navel and genitalia, but possibly the worst was the wound to her chest. It appeared that an amount of flesh had been cut away from the underneath of her left breast, but there was no sign of the missing flesh. Where was it? Had the killer taken it away with him as a souvenir? Doris' left hand was resting between the top of her legs, but it appeared to have been placed there by the killer, rather than something that she would, or could, have done herself.

Somewhat bizarrely, the knife that had been used to inflict the wounds to Doris' body had not only been left behind by the killer, but it had been placed on one of her thighs. At some time during the attack, her assailant had left the bedroom and gone to the kitchen to pick up a potato peeler, which he then used to carry out some of the mutilations.

One of the unusual aspects of the murder was that Doris' killer had possibly had sex with her twice before he attacked her. All the other murders or attacks had not involved sexual intercourse as the main driving force, as the sole purpose had been the actual killings. On each occasion, regardless of whether the individuals had been killed or survived, the attack was relatively quick, but with Doris he changed tactics. He had sex with her twice before he strangled her and then mutilated her body, but there had not been any attempt by the assailant to slit her throat, nor to insert anything into her vagina, as he had done with previous victims. This was unusual as he certainly would not have been in any rush; this was one attack where time was definitely on his side.

The unknown element of the frenzied attack on Doris Jouannet is whether she was alive or dead when he mutilated her body. Had her killer simply strangled her into a state of unconsciousness, mutilated her body then finished her off by pulling the stocking round her neck even tighter, until her life eventually ebbed away?

By now the thought must have crossed the mind of Detective Inspector Clare that the murder was connected to the spate of other murders and attacks which had taken place in the area, especially as he was also one of the police officers who was involved in the investigation into the murder of Evelyn Hamilton, whose body had been found inside the air raid shelter in Marylebone three days earlier, on 9 February.

As for Doris, her death that night was more than likely a direct consequence of her killer's failed attempt at murdering Catherine Mulcahy. It was only by killing Doris Jouannet that he had sated the beast within him for the night. If he had not met Doris on that cold winter's night, it is possible he would not have returned to his billet until he had killed somebody, no matter how long it took him.

It was after the murder of Doris Jouannet that the press gave the killer the nickname the "Blackout Ripper", immediately drawing direct comparisons with Jack the Ripper, the notorious killer of prostitutes in the East End of London during the late 1880s.

Margaret "Greta" Heywood

The police received another opportunity to discover the identity of the killer thanks to a woman by the name of Margaret "Greta" Heywood, who it would be fair to say allowed them to make their break-through in the case. On Friday, 13 February she met a man at the Trocadero in Piccadilly, a famous meeting place that included bars, restaurants and cabaret shows for its discerning guests to enjoy themselves in. After buying her a few drinks, the pair left the Trocadero together and made their way in the general direction of the West End's main theatre district, in the Haymarket. As they reached Piccadilly Circus, where Regent Street meets Piccadilly, suddenly, and without any warning, the man pushed Margaret firmly, but not aggressively, into an unlit shop doorway. He placed his hands on her hips but did not at that stage try to touch her sexually. She agreed to kiss him, but more to satisfy his continued persistence rather than any personal desire on her part. Her attacker, however, saw the kiss as a beginning and tried to convince and persuade Margaret to go with him to a nearby air raid shelter so they could continue their liaison in private. Guessing what he had in mind, she rebuked his suggestion, but his intentions became blatantly obvious and with caution now clearly thrown to the wind, he began groping and fondling her body. Realising the situation was starting to get out of control, she slapped at his wrists in an effort to break the grip he had on her, but still he persisted. Mustering all the strength she could find, she managed to finally push him off and started to walk away, but the danger was not over. With his blood now up, her attacker reached out and grabbed Margaret by the throat, pushing her backwards into the shop doorway as he did, before proceeding to choke and throttle her until she passed out. What exactly he intended doing to her once she was unconscious is unknown, but it certainly would not have been anything nice if his previous attacks and murders were anything to go by.

The obvious problem he had was that the two of them were outdoors and although there was a public shelter nearby, he would have had to pick her up and carry her, whilst hoping that he did not bump into anybody along the way, especially a policeman. Public, brick-built air raid shelters were easily identifiable because they were marked with a black 4-foot by 2-foot sign, with a large white S painted in the middle and the words "SHELTER" painted in white across the top and "HERE" across the bottom.

Fortunately for Margaret, when she passed out her assailant may well have assumed that he had, in fact, killed her. He now believed he had plenty of time on his hands, because his first thought was to begin rifling through her handbag and purse. Whilst doing so he was suddenly interrupted by a young delivery boy called John Shine, who was making a delivery to the nearby Captain Cabins pub in Norris Street. It was just before 10 pm when he heard what he thought was the sound of a fight and went to investigate. His intervention undoubtedly saved Margaret's life, as her surprised and flustered attacker panicked and ran off, using the darkness of the blackout as his cover.

As Shine approached the location of where he had heard the commotion coming from, he was obliged to light a match to be able to see better, because with the blackout in place, it was not so easy to see things or make out what was what. He was, however, quick enough to see the outline of a figure disappearing out of the other end of the alleyway, whilst at the same time spotting a woman's legs sprawled across the pavement by the doorway of a nearby shop.

The 18-year-old Shine ran to the woman's assistance, not knowing at that moment in time whether she was alive or dead. Much to his relief, however, no sooner had he reached her than she regained consciousness, although she was understandably in a state of shock at what had happened. Her skirt was raised up, almost around her waist, her face bloodied and her clothes were partly torn. Shine helped her to her feet, but she was far from alright, the attack certainly having taken its toll on her wellbeing and state of mind. Shine tried his best to try to find out what had happened, but initially Margaret's words were at best a mumble. Nevertheless, she quickly regained her composure and with it her voice. Her first concern was the whereabouts of her handbag. Shine knelt down, gathering up the contents of her bag which had been tipped on the ground and placed them back inside the handbag before handing it to her. Whilst doing so he noticed a gasmask and haversack in the doorway and asked if they were hers. When she replied they were not, he picked them up rather than just leaving them where they were. It seems that in his haste to escape the crime scene, her attacker had left a vital clue behind.

Being the polite and well-mannered young man that he was, Shine offered to accompany Margaret to hospital so she could have her injuries treated. The nearest one was Guys, about 2 miles away, and en route they bumped into a Metropolitan Police constable by the name of James Skinner, who had just started his nightshift and was out walking his prescribed beat. On seeing the couple, he had initially assumed that Margaret was drunk, as Shine was clearly having to support her so she could stay on her feet. Between them they explained what had happened. Recognising that Margaret's injuries were neither severe or life threatening, Constable Skinner, who would have no doubt been aware of the murders of Evelyn Hamilton, Evelyn Oatley, Margaret Lowe and Doris Jouannet, along with the attack on Catherine Mulcahy which had taken place across the district during the course of the previous few days, suggested that the initial priority might be for the two of them to accompany him to the police station in Savile Row, so that witness statements could be obtained in relation to the attack and assault.

Whilst Margaret, Shine and Constable Skinner were making their way to the police station, her attacker had remained in the area, finding a degree of sanctuary in the surroundings of a nearby pub. The realisation he had left behind his gasmask and haversack had already hit him, and he was in a bit of a quandary as to what he should do next. If the items were recovered, he was surly an intelligent enough individual to know that he could be identified from his personal regimental service number that was etched on his gasmask. He initially considered returning to the scene of the attack to see if both items were still there, but knew this was an extremely risky thing to do as the police might already be there carrying out their investigation, and already have possession of both his gasmask and haversack. In the end he decided that the best thing he could do was to steal a fellow airman's gasmask and then return to his billet His reasoning was that if he at least had one, albeit someone else's, he could certainly come up with a reasonable story as to how he had come to be in possession of it.

Back at Savile Row Police Station, Detective Sergeant Thomas Shepherd had already spoken with Margaret Heywood and taken a statement from her about the attack. He had also had the opportunity to examine the gasmask and would have seen the RAF regimental service number 525987 etched on the inside of the haversack. It was now just a matter of time before its owner was identified and arrested.

This was exactly the breakthrough the police needed, although when the matter was first reported, it may not have been obvious that this particular attack had been carried out by the same man who had murdered the four previous women.

Detective Sergeant Shepherd contacted the RAF Police at their headquarters at RAF Honington, but then had to sit and wait for them to phone back with a name. After making some enquiries, an RAF officer informed Detective Sergeant Shepherd that regimental service number 525987 had been allocated to Gordon Cummins, who at the time was supposedly on a pilot's course at Regent's Park. However, a quick check of personnel at the billets showed he was, in fact, not in his bed.

Maple Churchyard and Edith Eleanora Humphries

As well as the attacks mentioned above, it was later believed that Cummins was also responsible for two murders committed the previous year, in October 1941. Maple Churchyard was murdered on 13 October, her near-naked body being discovered in a bombed-out house at 225 Hampstead Road, between Bloomsbury and Camden Town, while Edith Humphries was found murdered just four days later, on 17 October, at her home at 1 Gloucester Crescent, Regent's Park.

The murder of Maple Churchyard came to light on the morning of Monday, 13 October 1941, when demolition workers arrived at 225 Hampstead Road, north-west London, by which time it was a bombed out and derelict property waiting to be pulled down. Whilst searching through the property, the demolition workers discovered the almost naked body of a woman, which later transpired to be that of Maple Churchyard. She had a bruise to the jaw and her suspender belt was pulled tightly around her throat and neck, but her throat had not been cut, nor had her body been mutilated. If she had been murdered by the same person who later attacked the women in February 1942, it was clear to see that over time he had become progressively more deranged in his actions.

Maple Churchyard had lived with her parents in Carleton Road, North London and was described as being an attractive woman, with a slim build, shoulder length black hair and a pretty face. She worked for the Hackney Corporation as a clerk in their electricity department.

On the evening of Saturday, 11 October, she met an old school friend who used to live in London, but because of the Blitz had moved with her parents to the more rural and less dangerous location of West Wickham, Kent. The girl and Maple had remained in touch after having left school and met up in London for a night out as often as they could.

The following evening, after going to the cinema, the two women made their way to Charing Cross station, where Maple's friend caught the 9 pm train back to West Wickham. The intention was then for Maple to catch a bus back to her home in North London, just over 5 miles away. It would appear that she did, indeed, catch the bus, but was attacked sometime after getting off and before she was able to make it home.

The other murder Cummins was later believed to have potentially committed was that of Edith Eleanora Humphries, who was found with her throat cut at her home at 1 Gloucester

Crescent, Regent's Park, London, on the morning of 17 October 1941. She had also been stabbed in the head; a blow which was delivered with such force that the knife penetrated her brain as well as her skull. She died in hospital the following day as the result of her injuries.

Edith was a widow and worked as a cook at the Auxiliary Fire Service station in Caledonian Road, London. She was of a friendly disposition and easy to get on with, this was borne out by the fact that she was known to have had a wide circle of friends, many of whom were men. There was no sign of any forced entry into the property, indicating that the person who attacked her was not only known to her, but somebody who she had possibly allowed into her home.

Edith was discovered by a neighbour from the flat above, who found her front door was slightly ajar and in darkness. The woman had lost her key and had gone to see Edith, who had a spare. She called out, but there was no reply. Instead, she heard the barking of her own dog coming from inside Edith's flat. The woman pushed the door open further, shone her torch in, and saw Edith laying on her bed in her night dress with blood all over her face. When the police arrived, they entered Edith's flat and discovered the neighbour's dog had been shut inside a cupboard. The neighbour was at a total loss to explain how this could be so, as when she had gone out she had left her dog locked in her own flat. It was also discovered later that several items of jewellery had been stolen from Edith's flat, the assumption being that the person who had murdered Edith had taken them.

Once the police had arrested Cummins for the four murders and two attacks in February 1942, they made further enquiries which led them to suspect him of having committed the murders of both

Church and Humphries. However, he made no admissions to the police of having done so, there was no solid evidence against him, and there were no known witnesses who had either seen him commit the murders or seen him in the vicinity of either of the crimes.

The only possible link that connects Cummins to either of these two murders is that on his visits to London, when he was on leave from RAF Colerne, the base where he was stationed at in 1941, he is known to have stayed at an address in St. John's Wood, which is believed to have been that of his brother. The distance from St. John's Wood to Regent's Park is just 3 miles, as it is to Hampstead Road (where Maple Churchyard was found), while the distance between Regent's Park and Hampstead Road is about 1.5 miles. This means that distance-wise it is quite conceivable for Cummins to have been in the areas of both murders if he was staying at the address in St. John's Wood at the time they were committed. Nevertheless, his movements whilst on leave throughout 1941 are not known, making any definitive connection between Cummins and the two murders impossible.

Chapter Three

Cummins' Arrest and Interview

Cummins was interviewed by Detective Sergeant Shepherd on the morning of 14 February in relation to the attack on Margaret Heywood. In essence, his story was quite vague. He admitted he had been out drinking the previous evening at the Volunteer public house with a colleague, but when asked for the name of the man in question, he could not remember it. He recalled catching a taxi with this man to Shaftesbury Avenue, where they began drinking at a bar in the Universelle Brasserie and consumed several more drinks, which included both beer and spirits. Sometime during the course of the evening, Cummins began a conversation with a woman whom he spotted sitting on her own, but he could not recall in any detail what their conversation had been about. The name of this woman was Margaret Heywood.

Shepherd did not ask, and Cummins did not state, whether he believed Heywood was simply a lonely woman looking for a bit of male company, or a prostitute looking to pick up a client. Indeed, there is no information or evidence to suggest that Heywood had ever worked as a prostitute.

Cummins added that he had a vague recollection of walking through the streets of the West End with this woman before ending up on his own in Piccadilly Circus, and realised he had passed the time when he was required to be back at his billet, so immediately hailed a cab and returned to his accommodation.

It was put to him by Detective Sergeant Shepherd that he had, in fact, attacked this woman, Margaret Heywood, causing her sufficiently bad enough injuries that she required hospital treatment. Cummins claimed to have no recollection of attacking Margaret Heywood, but then rather strangely apologised if he had hurt the woman, and even offered to pay her compensation. As his interview of Cummins drew to a close, Shepherd noticed that the knuckles of Cummins' left hand had cuts and abrasions on them. He enquired as to how the injuries had occurred, to which Cummins replied that he had injured himself whilst working on an aircraft engine.

Cummins was arrested on suspicion of causing grievous bodily harm to Margaret Heywood and remanded in custody whilst further enquiries into the matter were carried out.

Whilst in custody, detectives visited Cummins' billet where they checked the booking in and out records. These showed that he had signed out on the nights of each of the murders and attacks, but had returned on each occasion by 10.30 pm. Detectives also discovered that it was common practice for airmen staying at the billet to sign each other back in, meaning it was difficult to prove if someone had returned late. If men did wish to stay out, they could do so without actually signing in or out at all. The billet was also accessible via a fire escape, which meant that anybody could leave and return at any time they pleased without anybody knowing. This, of course, meant that the signing in and out book was not only pointless, but had very little relevance from an evidential point of view.

A search of Cummins' personal possessions at his billet produced sufficient evidence to connect him to the murders of Evelyn Oatley and Evelyn Hamilton, plus the attack on Catherine

Mulcahy, having already obtained sufficient evidence to charge him with the attack on Margaret Heywood. The pile of evidence against Cummins was added to further when his fingerprints were found to match those recovered from a piece of broken mirror found at the murder scene of Evelyn Oatley, and on the tin opener used to mutilate the body of Doris Jouannet. Meanwhile, mortar chippings, exactly the same as the ones discovered in the air raid shelter where Evelyn Hamilton's body was discovered, were found in Cummins' haversack. In addition, it was discovered that two of the £1 bank notes given to Catherine Mulcahy by her attacker had been issued to Cummins in his wages on Tuesday, 12 February. The net was most definitely closing in on Cummins, he just did not know how strong the case against him had become.

Detective Chief Inspector Edward Greeno of the Metropolitan Police arranged for Cummins to be placed in a police identification line up of eight men of a similar age, height, and general appearance, where he could be seen by the two women it was suspected he had attacked, Mulcahy and Heywood. The outcome of this line up was interesting, because despite Mulcahy having spent a considerable amount of time in a taxi, and at her flat, with Cummins, she was unable to pick him out as the man who had attacked her. However, due to the growing weight of evidence the police had against him, Mulcahy's inability to be able to identify Cummins as the man who had attacked her was of no great concern to Greeno. Margaret Heywood, on the other hand, immediately and without any hesitation identified Cummins as the man who had attacked her on Friday, 13 February.

Cummins was having none of it, and simply persevered with his claim of innocence, challenging Heywood's identification of him, even though he had admitted meeting and walking with her in the streets of the West End when he was first questioned about the attack. The more outrageous of his suggestions was that the attack had been carried out by another airman who, having previously taken his gasmask and bag, intentionally left it at the scene of the attack so as to cover up his own identity and, in doing so, make it look like it was Cummins who had carried out the attack.

In truth it did not really matter that Cummins made no admissions about having carried out the murders, because the police could now directly link him to a key piece of evidence believed to have been used in one of the killings, as well as recovering personal items from him which belonged to some of the murdered women. Although he tried to use the excuse that a colleague of his must have taken his RAF-issued gasmask, Cummins could have no plausible excuse for being in possession of the women's personal items.

Whilst on remand Cummins was held at Brixton Prison in South London, a trial and remand prison for those involved in pending cases throughout London and the Home Counties. On 16 February he had a visit not from a relative, friend or colleague, but from DCI Greeno, who was rather hoping that having had time to contemplate the situation he now found himself in, Cummins might just be prepared to make full and frank admissions about the women he had killed and attacked, not to mention explaining why he might have carried out these atrocious acts.

Greeno was particularly interested to hear about Cummins' movements between Monday 9 and Friday, 13 February, especially those which took place in the hours after he had finished his daytime commitments, all the way through until the small hours of the following mornings. Greeno did not receive the answers he was hoping for. Sat opposite him, and separated by a table, he set out photographs of the women who had been murdered and attacked, but Cummins remained emotionless. To each image placed in front of him, he simply shook his head and denied having ever seen or knowing them.

Greeno was not only an experienced police officer and detective, he was also a seasoned interviewer of criminal suspects who had committed all manner of different crimes. This gave him an innate ability at knowing when somebody was not quite telling him the truth, and although the usual tell tail signs were not so obvious with Cummins, the evidence Greeno had in his possession told him that the version of events Cummins was providing him with was nowhere near the truth.

Greeno produced and questioned Cummins about all the victims' personal items which had either been found on his person when he was arrested, or at his billet whilst he was in custody. Other than to say they had been in the haversack he had with him at the time of his arrest, which was, of course, not his, he had no further explanations.

If Greeno had been in any doubt about what he was going to do in relation to Cummins, their meeting, and more importantly the responses he received to his questions, determined what he should do. The following morning Greeno returned to Brixton Prison where he once again saw Cummins, but this time his reason for being there was simply to inform him that he was to be charged with the murders of Evelyn Oatley, Margaret Lowe and Doris Jouannet, and that he would remain incarcerated at Brixton Prison until the date of his crime.

Before Cummins appeared before the Central Criminal Court at the Old Bailey on 24 April, he had been further charged with the murder of Evelyn Hamilton and the assaults on Catherine Mulachy and Margaret Heywood.

Chapter Four

Cummins in Court

B efore his eventual trial at the Old Bailey, Cummins appeared several times at police courts. After each such hearing he was remanded in custody until his next court appearance, the main purpose being to provide the police with sufficient time to complete their numerous enquiries. Cummins first appeared at Bow Street Police Court on Tuesday, 17 February charged with the murder of three women in the West End of London. He was remanded in custody until his return to the same court on Friday, 20 February, where long queues formed outside the main entrance due to the large number of people eager to obtain a seat in the Public Gallery.

Cummins was not charged with the murder of Evelyn Hamilton at these proceedings, presumably because the police had insufficient evidence for this particular case, but in addition to the three murders he *was* charged with, he was also remanded in custody until 12 March for causing grievous bodily harm to Margaret "Greta" Heywood by striking her in the face and catching her by the throat at St. Albans Street, Haymarket on 12 February.

On Thursday, 12 March Cummins once again appeared at the Bow Street Court, where it was claimed that his fingerprints had been found on items at the apartment of Margaret Lowe, the second of the women he was alleged to have murdered. His prints were found on items including a drinking glass, a stout bottle, and a candlestick, and while this was most definitely a case where fingerprint evidence played a big part in the final outcome of the trial, it is very surprising that a man who could be so precise as to plan and commit such a heinous offence had not considered or taken steps to ensure such basic mistakes as leaving evidence were made. What is more, when he was arrested Cummins was found to be in possession of Margaret Lowe's silver-plated cigarette case.

When the prosecution opened their case relating to the murder of 42-year-old Evelyn Oatley, also known as Leta Ward, a statement from Cummins was read out. In it he said that he had never been in any other flat in the West End with another woman except Miss Laura Denmark, who was also in court to give evidence on Cummins' behalf. Miss Denmark was a blonde-haired prostitute whom he had met in Soho on the evening of 9 February. After going to her nearby flat, he had paid her for sex, but possibly due to the amount of alcohol he had already drunk, he was unable to complete the act. It was after he had left Miss Denmark's flat and returned to where they had initially met that he later supposedly encountered Evelyn Oatley. Cummins' defence team were hoping to show that this would prove he could not have possibly killed Evelyn, because at the time of her death he had been with Laura Denmark.

For the prosecution, Mr Vincent Evans told the court that Margaret Lowe's bedroom door was locked and had to be forced open by the police. On doing so they discovered her lying on her bed with a stocking tied tightly round her neck and throat. Her body had been mutilated, although the exact details of how were not repeated in the court. A broken poker and four blood-stained knifes were found on the bed close to or on her body.

A neighbour of Margaret Lowe's, Mrs Bartolini, gave evidence that in the early hours of 11 February, at about 1 am, she heard Margaret enter her flat, followed by somebody with heavier footsteps, indicating the likelihood this other person was a man. She later heard the person with the heavier footsteps leave Margaret's flat, although she could not be exact as to the time.

One of the witnesses produced by the prosecution was a fair-haired 15-year-old schoolgirl, who gave evidence that the cigarette case found in one of the pockets of Cummins' RAF tunic had belonged to Margaret Lowe.

Somewhat bizarrely Mr Evans asked the young girl, 'Was Mrs Lowe your mother?'

'I believed so, until a few weeks ago,' the girl replied in a low voice, adding that she had been living in the country but spent occasional weekends at Mrs Lowe's flat in Gosfield Street, where Margaret's body was found.

Mr Evans then moved on to the charge relating to the alleged attack on Margaret Heywood on the evening of 12 February. The couple had met in a bar and had entered into conversation with each other. They later left together and walked down some nearby back alleys. Cummins placed his gasmask in a doorway as he leant forward in an effort to try to kiss Mrs Heywood, but she resisted his advances. Mr Evans said that despite her response, Cummins persisted and whilst trying again to kiss her, he took hold of her tightly by the throat, gripping her so hard that she lost consciousness.

A passer-by, John Shine, heard some kind of commotion and went to investigate, and on doing so he saw a person shining a torch who, realising somebody was there, walked away, disappearing into the night. Shine did not see who it was, unable even to make out if it was a man or woman. He then escorted Margaret Heywood to the police station so she could give them an account of what had happened.

Because of the sudden and unexpected appearance of the good Samaritan passer-by, Cummins had to escape very quickly. In doing so, the court heard that a gasmask left behind at the scene of the attack had his RAF service number etched on its bag. Margaret Heywood had given Cummins her telephone number written on a piece of paper, which was discovered in Cummins' possession following his arrest. She also told the court that Cummins had shown her a sum of money from his wallet, which she estimated to be between £20 and £30.

It is quite amazing that after walking down a back alley late at night with Cummins, who was a total stranger to her, she seemed to be surprised when he tried to kiss her. While Cummins' actions are in no way excusable, it is hard to believe that Margaret Heywood was completely ignorant of the fact that some form of amorous encounter might have been expected.

Detective Sergeant Shepherd informed the court that when he interviewed Cummins, he had claimed to not be able to remember striking Margaret Heywood as he was very drunk and did not know what he was doing, but he was willing to pay her compensation.

Mr Evans also made mention of a fifth charge against Cummins, which was an accusation that he tried to strangle 22-year-old Catherine Mulcahy (also known as Kathleen King), at Southwick Street, Paddington, on 12 February. This was the first time this allegation had been mentioned in court, possibly suggesting that it had only come to light after the police had charged him with the other offences.

After Cummins was arrested, he was placed in an identity parade to see if the two women who had survived his attacks could recognise him. Margaret Heywood picked him out of the line up without hesitation, but Catherine Mulcahy could only say that his eyes were the same as those of her assailant. That she had specifically noticed his eyes would not have been that unusual in such a case, as the two would have been at very close quarters while she was trying her hardest to push him away, literally fighting for her life as she did.

After all the charges against Cummins had been heard by the court, he was further remanded in custody until his next appearance, which was scheduled for 27 March.

On that date, Cummins appeared before a judge at Bow Street Magistrate's Court. Having already been charged with the murder of three women, the attempted murder of one more and causing grievous bodily harm to another, he was further charged with the murder of Evelyn Hamilton between 8 and 9 February 1942.

The police had managed to gather sufficient evidence against Cummins to prove their case. This included a fountain pen with the initials of one of the three dead women engraved on it, which was, according to the prosecuting counsel, found in one of the pockets of an RAF tunic owned by Cummins. His fingerprints had been found on items belonging to two of the victims in their flats. A gasmask and its cloth bag with his RAF service number on had also been found in a West End street at the scene of one of the attacks, and an RAF belt, the same size as worn by Cummins, had been found in the flat of one of the victims.

Detective Chief Inspector Greeno gave evidence to the court that when Cummins had been charged with attempting to murder

Catherine Mulcahy at her Paddington Flat, he had replied that the accusation was, 'Absurd'.

Opening the prosecution's case in relation to the death of Doris Jouannet, who had been found strangled in her bed, Mr Vincent Evans said that it appeared Mrs Jouannet had led what could be classed as an "immoral life" while her husband was away working as a travelling salesman. Henri Jouannet was, in fact, the night manager of a London hotel. Maybe Evans had described him as a travelling salesman so as not to draw any unwanted attention to the hotel where Henri worked?

When the husband returned home after having worked a night shift, he discovered his wife in their bedroom with a stocking tied tightly around her neck, and her body mutilated. On the dressing table was a razor blade which had what appeared to be blood stains on it.

Mr Evans told the court that items found either in Cummins' possession or amongst his belongings had been identified as belonging to Doris Jouannet. Besides her fountain pen, this also included a comb and a wristwatch.

The court also heard from Flight Sergeant Raymond Smelus, who occupied a bed in the same room as Cummins. He stated that when Cummins returned to their room at about 4.30 am on 13 February, he said, 'Someone swopped my respirator and it's been found at the scene of some crime'. When questioned by police about the gasmask, he told Detective Bennett that he had picked it up in a West End brasserie where he had eaten, after somebody had picked his up by mistake and left theirs behind.

In relation to Evelyn Hamilton, Mr Evans outlined for the court how he believed Cummins had murdered her sometime either late on the evening of 8 February or in the early hours of 9 February.

He explained how her body was found in an air raid shelter in Montagu Place in Marylebone, after what appeared to have been a night out in London. Her handbag, which she was known to have been carrying, was missing. Mr Evans further added that on 8 February it was known by some of Cummins' fellow cadets that he was short of money, yet the following afternoon he showed a colleague somewhere in the region of £20.

Sir Bernard Spilsbury, the Home Office pathologist, gave evidence that in his professional opinion, Evelyn Hamilton's death was due to asphyxia caused by somebody who was either left handed, or who had used their left hand to commit the crime.

The prosecution's case was as complete as it was possibly going to be. The only thing missing were admissions from Cummins about having committed the murders and attacks, and why he had done so. But that aspect of the case was never going to happen.

Although complete, the case against Cummins was far from being watertight, with much of the evidence being circumstantial and the fingerprint identifications being challenged by Cummins' defence team.

Looking at the case today, it has to be said that the process was carried out with some haste. Cummins was arrested on 14 February and by 27 March he had already appeared at court on four separate occasions, with his trial date at the Old Bailey set for 24 April, just over nine weeks after he was first arrested. This was not some minor crime that was being investigated, it was an extremely complex case which included the murder of four women and attacks on a further two.

The backbone of the British legal justice system has always been based on fairness and the premise that an individual is innocent until proven otherwise. The speed at which the case against Cummins was dealt with appears to have been driven by an unknown force. The nation was at war and by 1942, public morale had been tested to the full. It is almost as if the British authorities wanted the murders of February 1942 to be solved and dealt with as quickly as possible, and for whoever was found guilty to face the maximum punishment that the law was able to provide. In this way the entire matter could be "put to bed" and the nation move forward as one in its efforts to defeat Nazi Germany and the Japanese Empire and secure overall victory in the Second World War.

Chapter Five

Trial at the Old Bailey

The trial of Gordon Cummins began in earnest on Friday, 24 April 1942 at the Central Criminal Courts of the Old Bailey in the City of London, with the distinguished Mr Justice Asquith, son of the former British Prime Minister Herbert Henry Asquith, presiding.

Cummins was brought up from the court cells and had to stand whilst the clerk of the court read out the indictment against him. Despite the weight of evidence, Cummins was only charged with the murder of Evelyn Oatley that had taken place on Tuesday, 10 February. The prosecution was clever in doing this because it was the murder of Evelyn Oatley that they believed provided the strongest evidence against Cummins, and it was the only case where they had fingerprints on two separate items found at the crime scene which they could claim belonged to Cummins. The problem for the prosecution was that they knew the evidence against Cummins for the murders of the three other women, Evelyn Hamilton, Margaret Lowe and Doris Jouannet, was nowhere near as strong, and could even be considered circumstantial. If Cummins was charged with all four murders, then the evidence in each case would have been discussed in great detail in court. The prosecution knew full well that if the jury had any doubt of Cummins' guilt in any one of these three murders, then their entire case could be jeopardised, and Cummins might well be found not guilty.

After the indictment had been read out in full, Cummins was asked how he pleaded. He replied, 'Not guilty'. The clerk then turned to the jury and informed them that once all the evidence in the case had been put before them, it was their job to determine if Cummins was guilty or not guilty of the crime he was charged with.

The Crown had employed a strong team to prosecute the case in the form of Travers Christmas Humphreys and G.B. McClure, both of whom were King's Counsels. The man appointed to defend Cummins was Dennis Nowell Pritt, also a King's Counsel. However, the case had little to do with how good or bad any of the barristers were; if ever there was a better example of a forgone conclusion, it would have been hard to find. The prosecution simply had so much damning evidence against Cummins it would not have made any difference at all as to who was defending him. Despite his not guilty plea, he was always going to be found guilty. The best Pritt could realistically hope for was to convince the judge to look favourably on a plea for clemency, in the hope that his client would be excused the hangman's noose.

Before the case could continue, Mr Justice Asquith decided that a new jury needed to be called because the initial one 'might be prejudiced' due to the fact that they had been presented with photographs of the deceased Margaret Lowe, who was not the person Cummins had been charged with murdering. The case was adjourned until the following Monday so that a new jury could be selected and sworn in.

With a new jury in place, the case re-commenced the following week on Monday, 27 April, but now Cummins had a new defence team consisting of John Flowers KC, and Victor Durand KC. To say Cummins appeared relaxed and at ease would be an understatement. It was hard to grasp looking at him that here was a man who was on trial for his life, especially when he could be seen smiling and waving to his wife. She was in the courtroom to support her husband; a loyal and loving individual who had convinced herself that Cummins was innocent and that the allegations against him were nothing more than a dreadful mistake.

The first witness called by the prosecution was Metropolitan Police Detective Chief Superintendent Frederick Cherrill, who was the universally accepted foremost fingerprint expert of the day. It would have been extremely difficult to have found an individual anywhere in the world who had such a high professional credibility in a particular field of evidence. It would have also been an extremely fool hardy barrister who would have dared challenge evidence Cherrill presented in court, and to have attempted to discredit him in any way would have done Cummins more harm than good. Cherrill was certain that the fingerprints discovered on the broken mirror and the tin opener, both of which had been used to mutilate the body of Evelyn Oatley, were a match to those of Gordon Cummins.

John Flowers, Cummins' counsel, did not disappoint when it came his turn to cross examine Cherrill, and decided to challenge his expertise and knowledge of fingerprints. This might not have been the best road to have gone down, especially when Cherrill's response was to state that he would stake his reputation on the fact that the recovered fingerprints were a match with those belonging to Gordon Cummins. As Cherrill's reputation as a fingerprint expert was impeccable, there was very little point in Flowers trying to push the matter any further.

If having Cherrill as a witness was not enough for the prosecution, they also had the luxury of putting Sir Bernard Spilsbury in the witness box to talk through the autopsy he had carried out on the body of Evelyn Oatley. He confirmed that the cause of death had been a deep cut to her throat and that in his estimation, she would have bled to death in under five minutes.

On the night of Evelyn Oatley's murder, Cummins had been out drinking with a fellow officer cadet from his course called Felix Sampson. This cadet also gave evidence to the court, on behalf of the prosecution, that on the night of Monday, 9 February he and Cummins had been out drinking in the West End. At some time before 11 pm, the two men found themselves in need of some female company. Outside the Monaco restaurant in Piccadilly, the pair met two prostitutes and because of the time frame involved, the woman Cummins left with was none other than Evelyn Oatley. The two men agreed to meet back at the same restaurant by 11.30 pm, after having spent some personal time with their respective companions. Sampson arrived back outside the restaurant at the agreed time, only to find Cummins was not there. Thinking that he was still enjoying himself, Sampson waited for half an hour but then left when Cummins failed to return.

Cummins, either of his own volition or by suggestion of his defence counsel, decided to give evidence in his own defence. Such a move has the potential to go badly wrong for a defendant as by doing so, they leave themselves open to be cross-examined by the prosecution. However, by not giving evidence, there is always a concern that undue inference could be taken by members of the jury.

Cummins had to take the stand because it was Evelyn Oatley's murder which had brought the fingerprint evidence into play.

His prints had been found on a piece of glass from a broken mirror and a tin opener, both of which had been used to mutilate her body. Whether he wanted to or not, he had to come up with some kind of explanation as to how his fingerprints had been found inside Oatley's flat, specifically on items that were used to mutilate her body. What could he possibly say? What plausible explanation could he come up with to explain away the presence of his fingerprints in Oatley's flat? When Detective Chief Inspector Greeno had interviewed him at Brixton Prison on 16 February and shown him photographs of all the victims, he had stated that he had never seen, and did not know, any of the women concerned.

Under cross examination he admitted having seen Evelyn Oatley on the night she was murdered, but added that she was alive and well when they parted company. Maybe realising that he would be pushed even further on the matter, he added that he was particularly drunk on the night of her death and was therefore unable to remember anything to do with actual timings of his whereabouts as he was not wearing a watch.

After all the evidence had been presented to the court, both the prosecution and defence counsels presented their closing arguments to the jury. After this, Mr Justice Asquith addressed them, with his summing up going on for more than an hour and ending with the following statement:

> *A sadistic sexual murder has been committed here of a ghoulish and horrible type, but of a type which is not at all uncommon, and that has been done by somebody. What you have to determine is whether, upon the evidence, it has been proved beyond reasonable doubt that the murderer was the*

man who stands in the dock. His life and liberty are in your
hands, but in your hands, also, are the interests of society.

Having listened to both the prosecution and defence counsels,
as well as the judge, all that was left for the jury was for them to
retire to consider their verdict. This was at 4 pm. By the time
they returned to the courtroom it was 4.35 pm. It had taken just
thirty-five minutes for them to make their decision.

Everybody held their breath as they awaited the verdict.
Cummins, with his heart pounding and beads of perspiration
across his forehead, tried as best he could to remain calm. The
twelve men of the jury filed back into the courtroom and took
their seats as an umbrella of silence quickly enveloped the tense
atmosphere which prevailed. The moment of truth had finally
arrived. 'The defendant will stand,' said the clerk of the court,
before turning to the foreman of the jury.

'Have you reached a verdict?'

'Yes, we have,' was the reply.

'Is it the decision of you all?'

'Yes, it is.'

'How do you find the defendant. Guilty or not guilty?'

'Guilty of murder.'

The deafening silence which immediately followed the verdict
was a mixture of shock and relief. All that could be heard was the
gasp of exclamation from Cummins' wife in the gallery as she
burst into tears. Cummins' response might have seen more of
a reaction if somebody had asked him if he wanted a cup of tea:
although he fully understood the magnitude and the gravity of the
words he had heard the foreman of the jury read out, he showed

no outward signs of emotion. Knowing what the jury's decision meant for him, his reply was to repeat his plea of innocence.

Justice Asquith donned his black cap, a plain square of black fabric, on top of his judicial wig, turned to Cummins and said:

> *Gordon Frederick Cummins, after a fair trial you have been found guilty, and on a charge of murder. As you know there is only one sentence which the law permits me to pronounce, and that is you be taken from this place to a lawful prison, and thence to a place of execution, and that you there be hanged by the neck until you are dead. And may God have mercy on your soul.*

On leaving the Old Bailey, Cummins was driven directly to Wandsworth Prison in south-west London to await his execution.

Three other charges of murder and two of attempted murder were allowed to "remain on file". In English law, this means that if the judge in the case agrees there is sufficient evidence for a case to be made against a defendant, but it is deemed not to be in the public interest for a prosecution to go ahead (usually because the defendant has either acknowledged or been found guilty of a more serious crime), then the matter is allowed to "remain on file", which allows the matter to be revived in the future if so required.

In Cummins' case, because he had been found guilty of one murder and sentenced to death, he could receive no higher punishment even if he had also been convicted of the other murders and attempted murders.

As was almost a common practice with individuals who had been found guilty of murder and sentenced to death, Cummins decided to appeal against his conviction. After all, if he wanted to stay alive, he had no option but to so.

On Monday, 8 June three judges sitting at the Court of Criminal Appeal heard Cummins' petition against his conviction and death sentence for the murder of Evelyn Oatley. The appeal was based on the credibility of certain fingerprints which had been produced by the prosecution at his trial.

Cummins' lead counsel, Dennis Nowell Pritt KC, produced folders for each of the judges containing photographs of the fingerprints in question so that they could clearly follow the points he was making and the criticisms about the validity of the prints.

On behalf of his client, Mr Pritt submitted that the jury's verdict was against the weight of evidence produced at the trial, and that the judge was not emphatic enough when it came to advising the jury that they had to make their decision based purely on the evidence that was produced in the courtroom. Mr Pritt further submitted that his client did not have a fair trial as the national newspapers reporting on the case stated that Cummins had, in fact, been charged with the murder of four women when he had not. This being the case, it would, Mr Pritt suggested, have been impossible for the jury not to have been influenced by these remarks when it came to making their decisions, which in turn was unfair on his client and had ultimately resulted in a miscarriage of justice.

This was a classic case of a lawyer "grasping at straws" that were not even there. There was no miscarriage of justice, the fingerprint and physical evidence the prosecution had provided proved beyond all reasonable doubt that Cummins was guilty as charged.

Having listened intently to Mr Pritt's comments and observations, Mr Justice Humphrey gave the judgement of the court, which was a dismissal of Cummins' appeal. As far as he and his two colleagues were concerned, they unhesitatingly took the view that the evidence put forward by the prosecution was overwhelming. This was especially true of the fingerprint evidence, which was vital and of deadly significance.

As Cummins rose from the dock to make his way back to the court cells, he turned and glanced at an unknown woman who was sat in the public gallery. It is highly likely that this was his devoted wife, who had stood by him since the day of his arrest and believed he was innocent of the charges against him.

Gordon Cummins was executed by hanging on Thursday, 25 June 1942 at Wandsworth Prison. The original date for the execution had been 19 May, but this was put back when the Deputy Under Sheriff for the County of London was informed by the Governor of Wandsworth Prison on 4 May that Cummins wished to appeal his conviction. The Home Secretary was informed of this decision the following day.

The execution was carried out by Albert Pierrepoint, who noted how calm Cummins was as he walked the short distance from his cell to the scaffold. There was no struggling or fighting against the inevitable. In Cummins he saw a man who appeared to have accepted his fate and was at peace with himself in the last few moments of his life.

Chapter Six

Cummins Hits the Headlines

There was, understandably, a great deal of media interest in the women Cummins was convicted of killing. Collectively, the various newspaper articles provide a flavour of the true magnitude of the crimes he committed and the lives of those he attacked and murdered.

The *Bradford Observer* from Wednesday, 11 February carried an article about the murder of Evelyn Oatley.

Former Keighley Girl Murdered

The mutilated body of pretty, blonde Evelyn Oatley, 32-year-old ex-actress, and a native of Keighley, was found yesterday in her room in Wardour Street, London.

Her husband, Harold Oatley, retired poultry farmer of Lyddlesdale Avenue, Blackpool, collapsed when told last night what had happened.

Before leaving for London to identify the body and to assist the police, he said that his wife was "fascinated by West End life and would not leave it," as her husband, Harold Oatley, told before catching the night train from Blackpool to assist police enquiries.

Detectives last night made a round of the Soho night haunts whose tinsel glitter drew the girl from Keighley to London and her death.

Clad only in a nightdress, her mutilated body was found yesterday on her bed with throat wounds, caused, apparently by a razor, though police have found no weapon. She was still wearing her jewellery.

Seeking Divorce

Nearby was the radio, which neighbours heard beating out dance music louder and later than usual toward midnight on Monday. Now they wonder if death came to Evelyn Oatley as it played, the blare muffling her cries.

Mr Oatley told a Press Association reporter that he visited his wife in London some days ago, returning to Blackpool on Tuesday last week.

"We did not live together," he said, "and I have recently seen a solicitor about a divorce."

It is about three years since Mrs Oatley left her husband in Blackpool and went to London, where in the name of Leta Ward, she rented the furnished one-room flat in which she died.

What is interesting here is it highlights just how fast moving such events can be. At the time, the only forms of communication were by radio, telephone, or handwritten or typed records, and if murders happened in different policing areas, they might not necessarily be immediately connected by the different police forces. It was abundantly clear that this was not the case with the four murders that took place in the West End of London in February 1942. Just three days after this article appeared, the same newspaper added to the story by reporting that two more women had been found murdered, not knowing at the time that they were all connected.

An interesting article appeared in the *Shields Daily News* on Friday, 13 February, which reported on a conference between Detective Chief Inspector Davies of New Scotland Yard, officers from Northumberland CID, and pathologist Doctor Cookson.

Their main topic of conversation was the murder of Mrs Susan Wilkinson of Sycamore Street, Ashington, in Northumberland, and that the un-named suspect in the case was believed to be a young soldier who was reported as being absent from his unit.

Doctor Cookson's report concluded that the attack on Mrs Wilkinson had been a surprise one and delivered from behind, but what was not made clear in the article was the relevance this murder in Northumberland had with the attacks taking place in London. Most likely, it was simply a case of senior officers within the Metropolitan Police trying to ascertain whether the murder of Susan Wilkinson was linked to those of Hamilton and Oatley, and whether there was a possibility that the same man had murdered all three women.

The article then went on to talk about Evelyn Hamilton and Evelyn Oatley.

Shelter Tragedy

Robbery is still believed to have been the motive for the murder of Miss Evelyn Margaret Hamilton, 41-year-old chemist, of Howlett Hall Road, Denton, Newcastle, who was found strangled in an air-raid shelter at Marylebone, London, on Monday.

Detectives are intensifying their efforts to trace her movements between 10.45 p.m. on Sunday, when she left a hostel in which she had booked a room, to walk to a café for a meal, and the time the crime was committed about midnight. Her handbag, rifled of its contents, was found in a garden near the shelter.

It is known that the handbag contained an identity card and ration books in the name of Evelyn Margaret Hamilton, and with a Hornchurch address, a square white metal petrol lighter, a wooden veneer cigarette case, 4 by 3 inches, marked by a number of cigarette burns, a round, white metal compact, a black fountain pen and a long nail file.

Flat Murder

Definite progress has been made by Divisional Detective-Inspector Gray in his investigation in to the murder of Mrs Evelyn Oatley, 25-year-old blonde ex-revue artiste, who was found murdered in her Wardour Street, London flat on Tuesday.

An early development is expected as the result of interviews with people in Soho who knew the girl.

Mrs Oatley, who had been living in the flat for three years, was found clad only in her nightdress with her throat cut.

The *Bradford Observer* newspaper from Saturday, 14 February carried the following article about the murder of two women in London.

Two More Women Murdered in London: Five This Week

The slashed and strangled bodies of two more women were found in the West End of London last night, the latest victims of the murder wave in the Capital. Five women have died this week. At least three have been discovered within an area of just over a square mile, and the theory that they were the victims of one strangler cannot be ruled out.

A woman found dead after being slashed and strangled in a flat in Sussex Gardens last night is believed to be named Doris Jouannet, aged 32.

The body was found when an entry was forced into a room of a flat. There were, it is believed, wounds on the body which may have been caused by a knife.

The victim's husband, who worked nights, returned home after finishing his shift, only to find the bedroom door was locked. On forcing in his way in, he sadly found his wife dead on their bed.

Only an hour or two previously the strangled body of a woman, understood to Margaret Campbell Lowe, had been found in a house in Gosfield Street, killed, it is believed, with a silk stocking.

Mrs Lowe was described by a neighbour as a middle aged, pretty brunette, always stylishly dressed. She had a daughter, aged about 14, who attended a convent school, and was evacuated to Bristol, but returned home some months ago.

Detectives made a minute search of the flat for clues under the supervision of Chief Inspector Greeno.

The article goes on to explain how on the Monday and Tuesday the previous week, two other women, Evelyn Hamilton and Evelyn Oatley, had also been found strangled in London. It also includes information about how the "provinces" police were investigating the circumstances of the death in Ashington of Susan Wilkinson, the wife of a local miner, who had been found dead on the Tuesday in a country lane not far from her home. It was believed that the cause of death was a blow, or blows, to the head. Although this information was part of the same article, it was unclear if the inference was that this was believed to have been another victim of Gordon Cummins, although it is hard to understand how that could possibly have been the case.

The following is a continuation of the article from the *Bradford Observer* from Saturday, 14 February, and is useful as it provides a detailed description of Cummins' appearance.

May Give Help

Police officers inquiring in to the death of Mrs. Oatley, are anxious to trace a man who may be able to assist them. He is described as between 25 and 26, 5ft., 8in., fresh complexion, chestnut or medium brown hair, wavy in front, frizzy at the crown, brown eyes, small mouth, thin lips, clean shaven, chin slightly protruding and pointed.

He was dressed in an electric blue overcoat with thin grey lines and square check with fairly large collar and belt, grey trousers and brown shoes.

This description would, in part, certainly describe Cummins, with the age, height, hair colour and being clean shaven certainly being a match.

Whilst researching this book I have only heard of Cummins wearing his RAF uniform, but it is, of course, completely conceivable that he did go out sometimes in civilian clothes, but it was the wearing of his uniform in wartime London that he would have seen as being a particular attraction to the ladies.

The police were obviously keen to show they were being proactive in discovering who was responsible for the murder of these women, especially as they had no doubt worked out it was the same man. History had shown if they did not catch the man quickly, not only would more women die, but there was every likelihood that the civilian population of the nation's capital would be struck with widespread panic and concern. Having a high level of public morale was particularly important in wartime, as it kept everybody focused on doing their bit for the country's war effort.

This eagerness to show progress was highlighted by an article in the *Shield's Daily News* of Monday, 16 February.

Murder Clues Lead Police to Provinces

Latest clues in the investigation of the murders of four women in the West End of London have led detectives from their chase in the Home Counties, to the provinces.

Women police officers wearing plain clothes are being used as decoys in the hunt.

The victims are:-

Mrs Doris Jouannet, aged 32, born near Newcastle, wife of a London hotel manager, found strangled in bed in Sussex Gardens, Paddington, on Friday.

Mrs Margaret Florence Lowe, aged 43, found strangled in her flat in Gosfield Street, also on Friday.

Mrs Evelyn Oatley, also known as Leta Ward, 30, blonde, discovered stabbed in her Wardour Street flat on Tuesday, and

Miss Evelyn Margaret Hamilton, aged 40, Chemist, of Newcastle, strangled in an air raid shelter in Montagu Place, Marylebone, last Monday.

Post Mortems

Sir Bernard Spilsbury on Saturday made post mortem examinations of the two latest victims. His information provided further assistance for the police on the chain of clues. Scotland Yard chiefs were in daily conference throughout the weekend.

The belief that one man is responsible for the murder of Mrs Jouannet, Mrs Lowe and Mrs Oatley was further strengthened by a review in detail of the latest evidence.

The police still wish to interview a man described as between 25 and 26, with brown wavy hair and brown eyes, and wearing a blue check overcoat.

Lat night C.I.C. men combed West End night clubs in their search for the man. The police are still looking for the knife or razor blade with which Mrs Jouannet and Mrs Oakley were mutilated.

It is thought probable that the weapon, and the key of Mrs Jouannet's flat, are still in the possession of their assailant.

Another article covering the same theme and which also named the four murdered women appeared in the *Bradford Observer* on the same day, Monday, 16 February.

Murder Wave: Yard Chief's Conference

Crime chiefs investigating the murder of four women in the West End of London, conferred at Scotland Yard and reviewed in detail the latest evidence yesterday.

They noted a strong similarity in all the crimes, but as yet are not completely satisfied that one killer was responsible.

The dead women, included three who were murdered within an area of just over a square mile, and two with a Yorkshire link.

The murders of 19-year-old Mabel Church, found strangled in a bombed house in Hampstead Road on 13 October 1941, and of Mrs Edith Eleanor Humphries, who died from head injuries at her home in Gloucester Crescent, Regents Park, on 17 October 1941, were also being considered.

Among the officers at the conference were Superintendent J Sands, Superintendent Yandell, Chief Inspector E Greeno, of Scotland Yard, and Divisional Detective Inspectors Clare and Gray.

Scientists at Hendon police laboratory are examining blood-stained garments, articles removed from the rooms in which the murdered women were found, and other clues.

It is clear from this article that the editor and/or one of the reporters at the *Bradford Observer* had certainly made a connection between the murders that took place in February 1942, and those of Churchyard and Humphries back in October 1941. What is not clear is whether the newspaper made the connection on its own accord, or whether it was directed down that path by officers of the Metropolitan Police Service involved in the case.

In fact, when the deaths of Maple Churchyard and Edith Humphries took place, Cummins was stationed at RAF Colerne in Wiltshire, about 7 miles north of Bath, so for him to have committed either, or both of their murders, he would have had to have been on leave at the time. This is a plausible theory because when Cummins was on leave, he was known to travel regularly into London. At the time his brother, who Cummins was known to visit, lived in a flat in Queen's Mews, Bayswater, less than 10 miles from where Churchyard was murdered. It was also a similar distance to where the body of Edith Humphries was discovered.

The murder of Maple Churchyard even made newspapers on the other side of the world, as this article from *The Argus* newspaper in Melbourne, Australia, shows.

Blitz Murders Riddle for Scotland Yard

Then came the murder of Mabel Church, 19, who was found naked except for a suspender belt, which had been used to strangle her in a bomb wrecked house in Hampstead.

Fingerprint experts have asked doctors to remove pieces of skin from her body in order to determine whether photographs will reveal any sign of fingerprints. The skin will then be analysed by a process evolved at the Hendon police laboratory.

As an interesting side note, the request by Scotland Yard detectives for skin to be removed from Maple Churchyard's body to try to establish if the fingerprints of an assailant could be discovered, was a first in the history of British crime.

There was still confusion about who was or might be responsible for the murders of Evelyn Hamilton, Evelyn Oatley, Margaret Lowe and Doris Jouannet, even on the very day that Cummins was arrested. The edition of the *Yorkshire Evening Post* dated Monday, 16 February, included an article that once again named the four women, but went on to theorise that the murderer was a soldier on leave because all the murders had taken place during a five-day period. The article also included the fact that the police were still looking for a knife or razor blade, which they believed had been used to kill both Mrs Oatley and Mrs Lowe.

On Tuesday, 17 February, an article appeared in the *Liverpool Echo* about a court appearance made by Cummins at Bow Street Magistrates Court.

Triple Murder Charge
Aircraftman In Court

Gordon Frederick Cummins, 28 years old leading aircraftman, was charged at Bow Street today with the murder of three women in the West End of London. The women were:-

Mrs Evelyn Oatley, also known as Leta Ward, aged 30, found stabbed in her Wardour Street, Soho, flat last Tuesday.

Mrs Margaret Florence Lowe, aged 43, found strangled in her flat at Gosfield Street on Friday; and Mrs Doris Jouannet, aged 32, wife of a London Hotel manager, discovered strangled in bed at Sussex Gardens, Paddington, on Friday.

Cummins was remanded till Friday. About three-quarters of an hour before the proceedings began, a police car with drawn blinds entered the yard of Bow Street Police Station, and several members of a small crowd, consisting chiefly of women, ran forward.

Queue Outside Court

Chief Inspector Edward Greeno, of New Scotland Yard, said that about 10 am today, at the rear of the court, he charged Cummins with the three murders. When cautioned he gave no reply.

The magistrate said Cummins was already due to appear before him on Friday on another charge.

There was a long queue outside the court, but only a few people were admitted.

The murders committed by Cummins were just fifty-four years after those committed by Jack the Ripper in the Whitechapel area of East London, meaning that there would have been people still alive who had lived through those events. The country was reeling from the effects of the Second World War, at a time when the nation had already seen tens of thousands of its civilian population killed and injured in German bombing raids across the nation, and had suffered the deaths of nearly 170,000 of its military, with nearly double that who had been wounded and a similar amount who had become prisoners of war. The last thing anybody needed was to know that there was a killer in their midst who, as it turned out, was a member of the military intent on murdering innocent members of the public; people who by their very nature, Cummins should have been trying to protect.

On Saturday, 14 March an article appeared in the *Aberdeen Press and Journal* concerning the three murders and two attempted murders that had been committed by Gordon Cummins.

An R.A.F. numbered respirator found in a doorway off Piccadilly, where an attack was made on Mrs Greta Heywood on February 12, was stated by the prosecution at Bow Street to have led to the arrest of L/A.C. Gordon Frederick Cummins (28), air cadet, who is charged with murdering three women in the West End of London, and with causing grievous bodily harm to two others.

The second charge of assault was mentioned for the first time yesterday, when it was alleged that after leaving Mrs Heywood in the doorway, Cummins met a Mrs Mulcahy, known as Kathleen King (22), went with her to Southwick Street, near Sussex Gardens, scene of the murder the following night, and endeavoured to strangle her.

The Eyes of the Man
An airman's belt was found in the room, and Mrs King told the court, "The eyes of the man look the same as the eyes of the man in the dock."

The woman found strangled and mutilated on the point of death between February 9 and 13 were, Mrs Evelyn Oatley, also known as Leta Ward (42), of Wardour Street, Soho; Mrs Margaret Florence Lowe (43), a brunette, of Gosfield Street, and Mrs Doris Jouannet (32), wife of a London hotel manager of Sussex Gardens, Paddington.

A fair haired fifteen-year-old school girl, questioned by Mr Vincent Evans (prosecuting) about a white metal cigarette case found by the police in Cummins tunic when he was searched in connection with an assault charge, said it belonged to Mrs Lowe, whom she had believed to be her mother until a few weeks ago, and with whom she had spent every third weekend on a visit from the country.

The school girl in question was Barbara Lowe, who attended a boarding school for girls in Southend-on-Sea, and who had unfortunately been the one who discovered her mother, Margaret's body.

The same article continued:

Telephone Number
On the night of February 12, said Mr Evans, Cummins and another air cadet had several drinks in the West End. He

took Mrs Heywood into a doorway, put down his respirator, and said he wanted to kiss her. Instead, he grasped her by the throat so tightly that she lost consciousness.

A piece of paper with her telephone number given to Cummins by Mrs Heywood, was later found in his possession.

Mrs Heywood, in evidence, said that when Cummins first started to press her throat he was muttering something like, "You won't, you won't."

Kicked in the Dark

Outlining the prosecution's case concerning the alleged assault on Mrs King, Mr Evans said that the electric light in the room failed, Mrs King managed to kick her assailant, screamed and roused the household.

Mrs King, a smartly dressed auburn haired woman, said that she did not know if Cummins was the man, but her assailant was an Air Force man. His eyes looked the same.

Cummins was remanded until March 26.

The article is interesting because it makes no mention of the fact that at the time they were attacked, some of the women were working as prostitutes. There is also no explanation as to why Catherine Mulachy was using the name of Kathleen King. There could have been a number of reasons as to why no mention was made of the women earned their living, but the most plausible one appears to be that the prosecution may have felt that their case would be undermined if it became publicly known, and openly admitted, that each of the victims had been working as a prostitute.

As we have seen, Cummins' court case was scheduled to begin on Friday, 24 April 1942, but had to be moved to the following Monday after the judge ordered the jury should be discharged after being inadvertently provided with the wrong documents. In this case, the documents in question were a number of crime scene photographs of the murder of Margaret Lowe, and as the charge against him was for the murder of Evelyn Oatley, the images were clearly prejudicial to Cummins' defence.

The *Birmingham Mail* newspaper from Friday, 24 April included the following article on the matter:

Wrong Document Shown to Jury
Stops Murder Charge Hearing
R.A.F. Man Accused

There was a sudden collapse of the hearing of a murder charge at the Old Bailey today when a wrong document was handed to the jury for inspection.

Mr. Justice Asquith ordered the jury to be discharged, and said the case would be reopened on Monday.

The case was one in which Gordon Frederick Cummins (aged 28), an R.A.F. cadet was charged with the murder of four women and the attempted murder of two others, all in the West End of London. The dead women were, Evelyn Oatley, Margaret Florence Lowe, Doris Jouannet, and Evelyn Margaret Mimilton [sic], and the two other women are Greta Haywood and Catherine Mulcahy.

Cummins, who appeared in the dock in the uniform of the R.A.F., pleaded not guilty to all the charges. Mr. G. B. McClure and Mr Christmas Humphreys were for the prosecution and Mr. John Flowers, K.C., defended.

Barrage balloons in the skies over London, where they stayed day and night during the blackout.

Nightlife in London still went ahead, despite the risks.

Above: Piccadilly Circus at night.

Below left: Blackout rules for householders, pedestrians and motorists.

Below right: An air raid warden indicates what times the blackout is in force.

WHAT TO DO IN —
BLACKOUTS

★ HOUSEHOLDERS
1. Stay at home.
2. Put out lights in rooms not blacked out.
3. Use no matches or lights outdoors.
4. Let no light escape from your house.

★ PEDESTRIANS
1. Walk carefully, don't run.
2. Keep close to buildings and away from curb.
3. Don't smoke
4. Use no matches or flashlights.
5. Cross streets at intersections.
6. Get under cover.

★ MOTORISTS
1. Park at curb — at once.
2. Put out all lights.
3. Seek shelter.

★ WARNING:
Emergency blackouts will be enforced by the police, assisted by Air Raid Wardens. Carelessness in observing these precautions may invite disaster.

DON'T GIVE 'EM A TARGET !

Air Raid Wardens
WANTED

Right: A poster promoting the recruitment of air raid wardens during the blackout.

Below: London was still attacked by German bombers during the blackout. Even churches didn't survive the night-time destruction.

AND THEY ARE WANTED
NOW

GET INTO TOUCH WITH YOUR LOCAL COUNCIL

Left: Gordon Frederick Cummins. Notice the piercing stare of his eyes.

Below: Aerial photograph of RAF Colerne, where Cummins had been stationed.

Above: A woman walking on her own during the blackout in wartime London.

Below left: Evelyn Hamilton in happier times, enjoying a day out by the river. She was to become Cummins' first known victim.

Below right: Lyons Corner House, Marble Arch, where Evelyn Hamilton is said to have first encountered Cummins.

 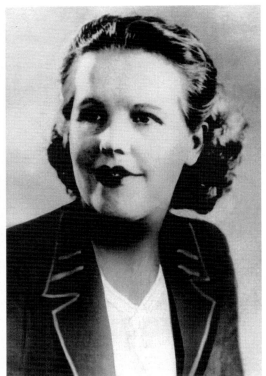

Above left: Inside a purpose-built air raid shelter, similar to the one where Evelyn Hamilton's body was discovered.

Above right: Evelyn Oatley, Cummins' second victim.

Below: Tin opener and women's hair tongs, similar to the types used to stab Evelyn Oatley.

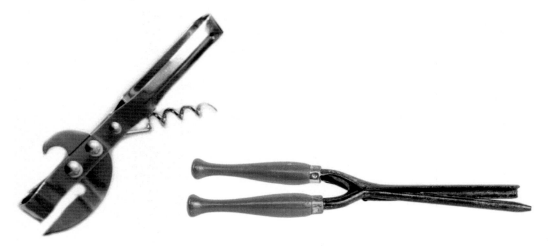

Above left: Cummins' final victim, the elegantly dressed Doris Jouannet.

Above right: The pathologist Sir Bernard Spilsbury, who carried out some of the autopsies on Cummins' victims.

Below: Detective Chief Inspector Edward Greeno (right) was one of the lead detectives in the case against Cummins.

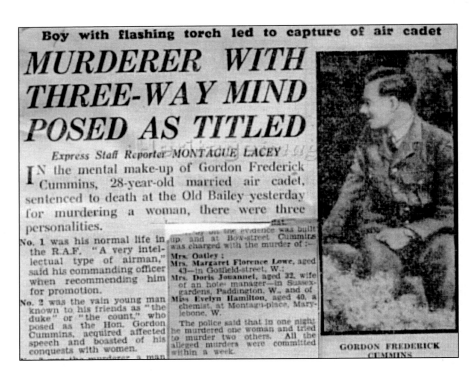

Clipping from a newspaper article, February 1942.

Wartime photograph of Wandsworth Prison, where Cummins was held before his execution in June 1942.

The reference to Evelyn Margaret Mimilton should, of course, be "Hamilton", and "Greta" was an alternative name for Margaret Haywood.

An interesting point in relation to Cummins' defence counsel, Mr John Flowers KC, is that three years after defending Cummins he was involved in another murder trial where the defendant was a Leading Aircraftman in the RAF, but on this occasion, he was the prosecution counsel against 38-year-old Arthur Heys, who had murdered a serving WREN, Winifred Evans. Heys was found guilty of murder and was hanged at Norwich Prison on 13 March 1945. In a further twist, Heys' father, Edward, had also been hanged thirty years earlier, aged 38.

On the prosecution was the somewhat controversial individual, Mr Christmas Humphreys who, as a prosecutor for the Crown, in 1950 was involved in securing the conviction and execution of Timothy Evans, who was wrongfully accused and charged of the murder of his young daughter, Geraldine. On 9 March 1950, Evans, having been found guilty of murdering his daughter, was executed at Pentonville Prison in Islington. John Christie, one of the main prosecution witnesses in the case against Timothy Evans, was later discovered to have murdered eight people, including his own wife, Ethel, and Timothy Evans' wife and child, at his home at 10 Rillington Place, before burying them in the rear garden as well as inside the house. Christie was subsequently sentenced to death by hanging, and went to the gallows on 15 July 1953, also at Pentonville.

Timothy Evans received a posthumous pardon for the murder of his wife and daughter, after his conviction for murder was quashed in 2004. Sadly for him, an action that was more than fifty years too late.

Humphreys was also the prosecutor in the infamous 1953 case of Craig & Bentley. On the evening of Sunday, 2 November 1952, 16-year-old Christopher Craig and 19-year-old Derek Bentley, who had been described as being "border line feeble minded", were in the process of burgling a warehouse belonging to a confectionary company in Croydon, South London. At the time, Craig had in his possession a .455 calibre Webley revolver. Having been spotted climbing over a gate to get into the premises, the police were called and Craig and Bentley were cornered on the roof of the building. After been told by Detective Sergeant Frederick Fairfax to hand over the gun, it is claimed by the police that Bentley was heard to say, 'Let him have it, Craig,' to which Craig responded by opening fire and striking Fairfax in the shoulder. Soon after this more police officers arrived and made their way up on to the roof. The first to make it was Police Constable Sidney Miles, who was immediately killed when he sustained a gunshot wound to the head after Craig had once again opened fire.

Both Craig and Bentley were charged with murder but because under 18s could not be sentenced to death, only Bentley was given the death penalty. It was a controversial decision because Bentley had not fired any shots and it was a point of debate as to whether he was mentally fit enough to even stand trial. A report written by Dr Hill, a psychiatrist from the Maudsley Hospital in South London, who had examined Bentley, described him as being 'illiterate, of low intelligence and almost borderline retarded'.

Craig and Bentley were both found guilty of murder, but despite a plea by the jury for clemency, the trial judge, Lord Goddard, sentenced Bentley to death. Bentley's legal team appealed the sentence, but their efforts were to no avail, and he was hanged at Wandsworth Prison on 29 January 1953. However, in 1993 he was given a posthumous pardon, and in 1998 the conviction was overturned.

In 1958 Humphreys was also involved in the prosecution and conviction of Ruth Ellis, the last woman hanged in the United Kingdom, after she was convicted of killing her lover, racing car driver, David Blakely.

The cases of Timothy Evans and Derek Bentley were both seen as miscarriages of justice, which resulted in both men being pardoned for the crimes which they had been convicted of, and along with Ellis' conviction, all three cases played a major part in the abolition of the death penalty for murder in the United Kingdom.

With Humphreys as the lead prosecutor in the case, Cummins and his defence team were up against a formidable and seasoned opponent, but to a degree it also questions the outcome of the Cummins case, as it could be argued that there was little in the way of cast-iron evidence to convict Cummins of the four murders.

Returning to the media coverage of the murders in February 1942, the *Birmingham Mail* described the events surrounding the murder of Evelyn Oatley:

> *The case concerning the death of Mrs Evelyn Oatley was proceeded with first. Mr McClure said that Cummins, a leading aircraftman and a cadet, was billeted in a large block of flats at St. John's Wood, London, Mrs. Oatley was a prostitute and occupied a flat in Wardour Street.*
>
> *Shortly after 8 o'clock on the morning of February 10, her dead body was found lying in her flat on a divan bed. Her throat and neck were cut on the right and her body had been mutilated. The discovery was made by some gas men*

who were examining a meter and they called the police. Near the body was found a blood-stained tin opener on which was a fingerprint. In a bag belonging to the woman was a mirror, also with a fingerprint on it. On the bag was found a blood-stained razor blade and a pair of curling tongs.

The handbag had been put in a cupboard, which was forced open. Usually it would have contained money, but no money was found.

Mr McClure said that the room in which Cummins slept at St. John's Wood had eight beds. There was a fire escape which permitted anyone to enter and leave at will without check.

Fingerprints Taken

When Cummins was arrested his fingerprints were taken and photographs were made of the left little finger and the left thumb. On the tin opener was a print of the left little finger and print of the left thumb was on the mirror. An expert would say that the prints were the impressions of the finger and thumb of Cummins.

The accused made a statement in which he said he spent the evening of February 9 with another cadet in the West End visiting bars and a restaurant, where they had dinner and a certain amount to drink. They met two women and decided each to go with one, and made arrangements to meet again somewhere in the vicinity of Piccadilly, but they did not meet.

Mr McClure remarked that Cummins boldly said that they did meet at 10 o'clock, an hour before they met the two women. That, said the counsel, was totally untrue, and the jury might think it was intended to provide a false alibi.

*The cadet with whom Cummins went to the West End
had said that he went to meet him at 11.15 pm as arranged,
but there was no sign of him. This cadet got back to the
billet about 6 o'clock in the morning and Cummins was then
in bed asleep. He woke him up and asked him why he did
not meet him, and accused said he went off with another
woman.*

*On the body, counsel continued, Sir Bernard Spilsbury
found 12 mutilations which could have been done with such
an instrument as a tin opener. A cigarette case belonging
to the dead woman was found in a refrigerator adjoining
Cummins' billet.*

On Tuesday, 9 June, an article appeared in the *Hartlepool Northern
Daily Mail* covering Cummins' appeal against his conviction for
murder.

"Vital and Deadly" Evidence
R.A.F. Cadet's Appeal fails

*Three Judges hearing the appeal of Gordon Frederick
Cummins, 28 year old R.A.F. cadet, against his conviction
and sentence of death for the murder of Mrs Evelyn Oatley in
her West End of London flat, studied finger print photographs
in the Court of Criminal Appeal, London, today.*

*Folders of the photographs were handed to them to enable
them to follow criticisms of the fingerprint evidence at the
trial made by Mr D. N. Pritt, K.C., Cummins,' leading
counsel.*

*As he entered the dock today, Cummins smiled to a woman
at the back of the court.*

Mr Pritt submitted that the jury's verdict was against the weight of evidence. He said that the Judge was not emphatic enough in his warning to the jury that they had to decide the case on the evidence alone. All the newspapers had been telling anybody who might be put on the jury that Cummins was charged with four murders.

Giving the judgement of the Court dismissing the appeal, Mr Justice Humphreys said they unhesitatingly took the view that the evidence was overwhelming.

The finger-print evidence was vital and of deadly significance. The summing up was unimpeachable.

Cummins glanced at a woman in court, and walked steadily out of the dock to the cells.

With Cummins having lost his appeal there was only one possible outcome, and it was now a matter of when and where the original sentence would be carried out. The day of his execution was set for Thursday, 25 June 1942, at Wandsworth Prison, and the events were recorded in the *Coventry Evening Telegraph* of the same day.

R.A.F. Cadet
Executed

Gordon Frederick Cummins, 28 years old R.A.F. cadet, who has been described as the most notorious killer since "Jack the Ripper", was executed at Wandsworth Prison today.

He was sentenced at the Old Bailey on April 29 by Mr Justice Asquith for the murder of Mrs. Evelyn Oatley (32), former revue actress, in her flat in Wardour Street, London. Three other charges of murder and two of attempted murder, were allowed to remain on file.

Cummins who was married joined the R.A.F. in 1935.

Several petitions had been made for a delay in the execution on the ground of other evidence, but officially it was held that there was no reason for interference with the sentence.

By March 1942, the Blackout Murders, as they had become known, were over, and the man responsible for them had been captured and was due to stand trial for what he had done. However, interest in Cummins and the murders he committed did not stop with his execution. The fascination in his crimes continued after the war, all the way through to the present day. At the time they understandably caused outrage, disgust and disbelief, but during the war years dramatic events were taking place nearly every single day, so one day's news really did become the next day's chip wrapper. The day after the body of his last victim, Doris Jouannet, was discovered, an estimated 90,000 British and Commonwealth soldiers surrendered to the Japanese in Singapore. On 19 February 1942, 243 Australian civilians were killed in Darwin, Australia, when the city is bombed by an estimated 250 Japanese aircraft.

London must have been an interesting place to be as the war entered its fourth year. Single women, or maybe even married women whose husbands were away fighting in the war, would have flocked to the nation's capital looking for a good night out. The number of smartly dressed, fit young men looking resplendent in their military uniforms and wanting to have a good time would have greatly increased following the arrival of the first American military forces in January 1942, just weeks before the first of the Blackout Ripper murders took place.

With Britain's young men involved in fighting in both Europe and the Far East, and with the civilian population having endured and survived nine months of the Blitz throughout cities across the nation, many people embraced the idea of living for the moment, never knowing what was around the corner. As for money, with so many Americans and other military personnel also enjoying the night life, many were always more than happy to buy a woman a drink or two.

The World's News dated 29 September 1951 included an article by New York writer, Spencer Hardy, in which he described life in London at the time of Cummins' crimes:

> *Something extraordinarily sinister crept in to the night life of blacked out London, especially in the vicinity of Piccadilly Circus, with its crowds of pleasure seeking servicemen, early in the wartime year of 1942.*
>
> *A woman killer was abroad in the streets, a misogynist as murderous as Jack the Ripper, who had spread terror in the same city in 1888 and 1889.*
>
> *Considering the rapid rate at which his crimes were committed, this new monster could have been expected to have been expected to have taken even more lives than the ripper did if he had not been tracked down so soon.*

It is likely that the number of Cummins' victims would have been more if it had not been for the fact that on the Wednesday evening of the week of his killing spree, he had to carry out guard duty at the Air Crew Receiving Centre in Regent's Park and was therefore unable to go out into town.

Hardy's article then looks at each of the victims, but does not include the additional two murders that took place in October 1941, which Cummins was later suspected of having committed. Indeed, it only looks at the four deaths and two attempted murders which took place in London in February 1942.

> *The first victim was a young unmarried woman named Evelyn Hamilton, a well-behaved pharmacist's assistant who had just quit her job in a drug store, announcing she was going to a new position in the sea port city of Grimsby. When last seen, she had been walking along Oxford St., in the Marylebone section, going to a restaurant for her supper.*
>
> *She would have never spoken to a strange man, which is more than could be said for the other women who died at the hands of her killer.*
>
> *On the morning of Monday, February 10, two workmen, preparing to make repairs to a bomb damaged section of street, stepped in to a concrete air raid shelter to get some sand from a pile they had left there. Inside the shelter they found the body of Evelyn Hamilton.*
>
> *Sir Bernard Spilsbury, the Home Office pathologist, examined the body and said that death had occurred the night before, that the young woman had been strangled by some man, apparently left handed, judging by the marks on her throat, who apparently had grabbed her in the darkness and dragged her in to this place.*
>
> *One motive that suggested itself was robbery. The victims' handbag was missing. However, her wrist watch had not been taken. It was the means of her identification. For her name was inscribed on it. There had been no sexual attack.*

Although Sir Bernard was revered as the founder of modern forensics, he also had his critics. His peers were not impressed with his desire to work on his own and his absolute refusal to train others. There were also concerns that juries were more readily persuaded by his courtroom arguments due to his celebrity status, rather than for the exactness of his professional assessments.

On the next morning, an electric meter reader visiting the apartments near Piccadilly Circus, discovered the death of young Mrs. Leta Ward.

Surprised that though the door was ajar no one answered his rappings, he had peered in and seen the body clad only in a sheer night gown, laying on a day bed which occupied the centre of the room.

The victims' throat had been cut with a safety razor blade and she had also been jabbed viciously and senselessly with a can opener and a curling iron.

Sir Bernard, called again, said that she had died some hours before, during the night. She had been strangled in to unconsciousness, and then her throat had been cut, bringing death. Someone had emptied her handbag of its money, scattering the other contents about. For London, killings like this, two nights running, constituted a crime wave.

Leta, a voluptuous blonde who had been a showgirl before the war, was not known to have enemies. Indeed, perhaps her trouble was that she had made too many friends. Apparently one too many, at any rate. Her husband, a travelling salesman, had been in northern England for the past six days, calling on customers.

> *A girl occupying the adjoining apartment said she had stepped out on the stair landing about 11.15 the night before and had seen Leta and a man in civilian clothing entering Leta's apartment.*
>
> *Scotland Yard found the print of a man's left little finger on the can opener, but it didn't match any print in the Yard's files.*

The comment about finding a man's fingerprint on the can opener is interesting, because at the time it was impossible to distinguish between a man and a woman's fingerprint. Indeed, this distinction only came about in 2015, when Jan Halamek, a forensic scientist at the State University of New York, and his colleagues tested fingerprints on different surfaces, which resulted in them discovering that it was possible to tell whether they belonged to a man or a woman by testing levels of residual amino acids in the fingerprints, which are twice as high for a woman than they are for a man.

The article then proceeded to describe the murder of Margaret Lowe:

> *The next victim was a young widow, Margaret Lowe. Neighbours were aroused to investigate on Friday by the howling of Margaret's Scottish terrier inside her locked apartment, on Gosfield St., in the West End.*
>
> *Constables who broke down the door found her lying on her bed, nude and lifeless. She had been killed the previous Tuesday night by someone who had strangled her first with a stocking and then cut her throat with a razor blade.*

Three hours after this discovery, and not two miles away, the night manager of a hotel, hurrying home to his young wife, discovered the fourth death. The apartment seemed strangely silent and deserted. He tried the bedroom door, it was locked.

Again constables were summoned and a door broken open. There on the bed, clothed only in an outflung dressing gown, lay Mrs Doris Jouannet, the hotel man's pretty wife, dead since a few hours after he had left her the previous evening when she had walked with him to his bus stop.

A stocking had been knotted and drawn tight about her neck, and her throat had been cut with a razor blade.

It is interesting to note that Margaret Lowe, Leta Ward (Evelyn Oatley) and Doris Jouannet had all been strangled and then had their throats cut, whilst Evelyn Hamilton had "only" been strangled. This could possibly suggest that in Hamilton's case, Cummins was disturbed before he had time to do this.

As Jouannet wept with a dual grief, for the death of his wife and the death of his faith in her fidelity, a detective asked him, "Do you know of any man who would have come to visit your wife while you were gone?"

"No," sobbed Jouannet. "I never dreamed of such a thing. We had been married six years and had always been happy together, I thought."

Though money had been stolen in the course of these crimes, the accumulated evidence pointed toward the assumption of some sexual psychopath to whom murder had become a substitute for ordinary love-making.

The comments included in the 1951 *World's News* article are backed up by modern psychologists. According to *Psychology Today*, 'The psychopath is sexually motivated by power, everything is a means to an end. If having a sexual relationship with a woman means that she will then trust him more or give him more money, he will perform the sexual task with Herculean bravado.'

Psychologists agree that psychopaths committing sexual homicide are motivated by hatred. J. Reid Meloy, a forensic psychologist, has argued that many sexual homicides are displaced matricides driven by maternal hatred.

A good example of this can be found in the case of Ted Bundy, the American serial killer who kidnapped, raped and murdered a number of young women and girls across seven states between 1974 and 1978, eventually admitted to having committed thirty murders, but the actual figure is believed by some investigators to have been much higher. Bundy was both handsome and charismatic and would often approach his victims in public places, knock them unconscious and take them to secluded locations to rape or strangle them. It was said that he selected victims who reminded him of his mother.

Meanwhile, the *World's News* article proceeded to discuss the attack on Margaret Heywood.

This was borne out by incidents that occurred last week on Thursday night. Like the murders, the incidents took place near Piccadilly Circus.

In the first case, a delivery boy carrying some wine to a night club heard a girl's strangled cry in a dark doorway. He swung his flashlight in that direction. A girl sank to the ground, and a man vanished in to the darkness. At a nearby police station, the girl, having recovered somewhat from her hysteria, told her story.

"I met an RAF cadet in a pub," she said, "a handsome chap. After some drinks together, we went out and walked down the street, and he was making love to me when suddenly he grabbed my throat with his left hand and began strangling me."

A little later, at about midnight, another girl reported having just had an almost identical experience with a good looking RAF man. He had started strangling her and had been frightened in to running away when she broke loose and screamed.

And still a little later, as was to be discovered, Doris Jouannet was strangled and slashed.

It is clear from those last three paragraphs that the compulsion which had enveloped him on that Thursday evening was all consuming and all powerful, and he did not stop until his desires had been sated. Despite having been nearly caught on two occasions, and despite being in RAF uniform, a factor which would not only have made him stand out, but would have helped the police to trace him, Cummins was unperturbed, and did not stop until he had murdered Doris Jouannet. The recklessness of his actions on that Thursday showed just how all-consuming his desire to fulfil his needs had become.

The article describes how, 'A detective was taken to the dark doorway where the first strangling occurred, and there he found an RAF gas mask and carrying bag. On the bag was stencilled the name Cummins and the serial number 525987.'

From an evidential point of view, it does not get much better than that. Although not completely conclusive, it was certainly a very good indicator that the police had their man and, at the very least, it gave them an excellent lead.

> *Though it was the middle of the night, Chief Inspector Edward Greeno of Scotland Yard put through a telephone call to the personnel records section of the Air Ministry and asked what could be learned from the gas mask clues.*
>
> *There was a quick check into the files, and the Chief Inspector was informed that the gas mask apparently was one issued to Aircraftsman Gordon Frederick Cummins, a new 28 year old cadet stationed temporarily at the Receiving Centre for Air Cadets in St. John's Wood, London.*

The police now had a confirmed name for their suspect and address where they could expect to find him. The race was on to locate and catch him before he could kill again.

> *Greeno then telephoned to the guardroom of the receiving centre (a group of apartment buildings converted into military billets) and asked that a check be made to see if Cadet Cummins was in his bed.*
>
> *A guard complied with this request and telephoned back that the cadet apparently had slipped out for an evening in town. Greeno requested that the cadet be detained for him when and if he arrived.*
>
> *At 4.30 am, Cummins returned to his quarters and went happily to bed and to sleep, undisturbed by the news that someone from Scotland Yard was coming to talk to him.*

Cummins certainly was a calm individual. He must have known, or at least had a very good idea, why the police wanted to talk with him. A normal reaction would have been to run and hide, which in a time of war, with the capital city being attacked on a regular basis by the German Luftwaffe, would not have been beyond the realms of impossibility. But then it would be fair to suggest that Cummins was not a normal person; he was quite possibly a psychopath, and as such would have had no moral compass, maybe even seeing himself as being smarter than those trying to catch him.

Officers at the receiving centre soon had marked as a good man for the King's commission and predicted he would go through the course of training with ease and distinction.

Cummins' fellow cadets had a different idea. They had marked the handsome aircraftsman as a phony. They didn't like his imitation Oxford accent and they didn't believe his story that he was the illegitimate son of an earl and rightfully should be called "the Honorable" Gordon Cummins.

And during this particular week of the strange killings, Cummins had annoyed his fellow flying students with stories of the big spending he had been doing in night clubs.

Later, it was seen that he could have been spending rather lavishly for a £2 a week cadet, considering what was taken from the handbags of murdered women.

The uneventfulness of Wednesday night, when no women were strangled or murdered, was explained by the fact that Cummins had been on guard duty that night. The two girls who had escaped attempted stranglings on Thursday night positively identified the cadet as their assailant.

> *Close examination of his gas mask carrying bag showed*
> *that it contained sand that exactly matched that in the pile*
> *where Evelyn Hamilton's body was found. The fingerprint*
> *on Leta Wards' can opener was proved to be his.*

The discovery of the sand and fingerprint which helped directly connect Cummins to both the victims was truly excellent work, as the time this forensic side of policing was nowhere as near as advanced as it is today.

> *Early on the night of Leta Ward's death, he had, he was able*
> *to prove, been with another girl. He said he had gone to this*
> *other girl's apartment and straight back to his billet from*
> *there, never meeting any such person as Leta.*
>
> *But apparently he had been inside two apartments that*
> *evening. In describing the interior of that flat he claimed*
> *to have spent the whole evening in, he got mixed up and*
> *described the arrangements of Leta's place, with the sofa bed*
> *strangely situated in the middle of the room.*
>
> *He was further incriminated by the discovery among his*
> *effects of cigarette cases and various other articles which had*
> *belonged to the murdered women.*
>
> *He was tried for and convicted of murder and hanged at*
> *Wandsworth jail. He never explained his sudden displayed*
> *lust for the killing of women.*

Why or how Cummins changed from being a normal, sociable individual into a rampant serial killer is something that will never be known. Even eighty years after he committed his horrendous crimes, interest in the murders, and the man behind them, is still rife. At the time, Cummins' reign of terror was both national and international news and gripped the imagination of the general public, who were left wondering where and when he would strike again. Thankfully, ongoing interest in the case helps to ensure that the names of those he brutally murdered and attacked have not been forgotten. It is most definitely a case which appears not only to have captured the imagination of the general public at the time, but continued to do so in the years that followed.

Chapter Seven

The National Archives Documents
in the Cummins Case

T he file relating to the case of Gordon Frederick Cummins, which is held at The National Archives at Kew, consists of 296 pages, and covers interviews, correspondence, and statements. While the entire contents of these documents will not be included here, an important selection will be analysed with the intention of uncovering certain interesting issues of the case that have not previously been widely discussed.

Document #1 of the file is a photograph of the folder's front cover, which contains all the file documents. What is interesting about this is that in the top right-hand corner of the page is a square, green sticker which says, "Closed Until 2043". However, there is nothing available which provides a date for when the early release of the file was approved, nor why it was released early in the first place.

Documents #5 and #6 relate to a meeting that took place on 18 June 1942 between the prosecution's legal representatives and Cummins' solicitor. The documents consist of a hand-written note on the prosecution's case file dated 21 June 1942.

Both Sir A Hardinge and I formed the impression at the time that the solicitor was genuinely convinced of the prisoner's innocence of the crimes with which he has been charged and

*in particular of the murder of Evelyn Oatley of which he
has been convicted.*

*But the solicitor's whole case focuses on a denial that
the fingerprints found at the scene of the murder of Evelyn
Oatley were those of the prisoner (though the fingerprint
experts at N.S.Y have no doubt that they are), and on
the suggestion that the cigarette case found in a kitchenette
cubicle at Cummins' billet at St James' Close was placed
there either by the real murderer (who was not Cummins)
or by the Police. Needless to say the Police indignantly
repudiate the suggestion that they fabricated this evidence
against the prisoner, and it is incredible that they should have
found the cigarette case on the premises of the deceased and
subsequently placed it a room near the prisoner's quarters.*

*On the other hand, it would be a coincidence of the most
extraordinary character if the civilian who was with Mrs
Oatley at one stage of the evening, had picked out the
prisoner's billet in which to hide the cigarette case.*

*I can find nothing in the solicitor's representations to show
any real, as distinct from a fanciful hypothesis, doubt on the
view of the jury and the CCA as to the prisoner's guilt on
the charge of which he has been convicted.*

This statement was obviously in relation to the appeal against
Cummins' conviction for the murder of Evelyn Oatley, as his
execution was carried out at Wandsworth Prison by Albert
Pierrepoint on 25 June 1942.

As for the reference to Sir A. Hardinge, his full title was Major
Sir Alexander Henry Louis Hardinge, 2nd Baron of Penshurst MC,

who at the time of Cummins' trial, besides being a King's Counsel, was also the Private Secretary to the king himself, George VI.

Document #9 is a typed Metropolitan Police report from Detective Chief Inspector Edward Greeno, dated 22 June 1942 to an unnamed Superintendent.

On 22ⁿᵈ June 1942, I received a further message from Mr. F.A. Newsam, Home Office, to the effect that another Petition had been received relative to the case of Cummins, alleging that after the latter had been arrested he was questioned by Police as to whether he was in Brighton about ten years ago, the suggestion being that he may have been responsible for the 'Brighton Trunk Crime'.

Detective Inspector Jeffrey, 'C' Division, interviewed Cummins and obtained his antecedence history, and declares at no time did he (Jeffrey) refer to Brighton or any crime committed. I certainly did not question Cummins as is alleged, and other officers engaged with me declare likewise.

No further prints were found by Police during the investigation or the 'Brighton Trunk Crime'.

In the case of Oatley, the wound in her throat was inflicted when she was at the point of death, no blood spurted therefrom, but only flowed from one severed jugular vein.

In the case of Lowe, wounds upon her body were inflicted after death, blood flowing only on to the bed from the wound in the right thigh.

The wounds were also inflicted after death in the case of Jouannet, blood flowing only from the wound in the left thigh.

> *In all cases it is possible that a little blood only might have got on to the hand used by the assailant when inflicting the wounds.*
>
> *I ask that a copy of this report be forwarded to His Majesty's Secretary of State to Home Affairs, Home Office.*

[Signed] *Greeno, Chief Inspector.*

The reference to the "Brighton Trunk Crime" relates to the dismembered corpses of two women left in large trunks in Brighton, in 1934. One of the victims remains unknown to this day. No one was ever convicted of either murder, although a bouncer by the name of Toni Mancini was tried for the murder of the second woman, Violette Kaye, with whom he had been in a tempestuous relationship. However, Mancini was found not guilty of her murder and acquitted. In 1976 Mancini admitted to a *News of the World* reporter that he had, in fact, murdered Kaye during a blazing row, in the course of which she had attacked him with a hammer. As there was no corroboration of Mancini's admission, it was decided not to prosecute him for perjury.

Document numbers #13, #14 and #15 make up the three-page typed statement, dated 19 June 1942, taken by Detective Chief Inspector Edward Greeno from an unknown woman living in Paddington. Both her name and address have been redacted. The first thing that is striking about this statement is not its contents, but the date; 19 June 1942. Cummins' trial at the Old Bailey took place over two days, from 27-28 April. Following his conviction, he appealed this decision, an application which was heard and rejected by the Lord Chief Justice on 9 June, and was hanged at Wandsworth Prison on the morning of 25 June. The obvious question is why take a statement from a potential witness six days before Cummins' execution, and ten days after his appeal had been heard and rejected?

> *STATEMENT OF [Name and address redacted]*
> *I am a married woman with two children, ages 5 and 3 years, a girl and a boy. They are living with my mother, but I do not want to give her address.*
>
> *My husband has been away working for the past three years and supports me.*
>
> *I am [at] present employed [as] a ledger clerk and typist, but I do not desire to give the name and address of the firm who employ me.*
>
> *In February 1942, I was out of work and during that month I used to meet men by appointment, in the Piccadilly area. Infrequently men used to accompany me home to this flat.*
>
> *I was in the Piccadilly Circus area in the early hours of the morning of 13th February 1942, I had previously been in Lyons Corner House and I walked across to the 'Monico' restaurant which has a big clock outside to see the time. To the best of my recollection it was a few minutes to or after two in the morning. I think it must have been just after two as I was just about to call a taxicab to go home. I think I may have been standing outside Swan and Edgars in Regent Street, after seeing the time, when an Air Force man in uniform came up and spoke to me. He said to me, "Which way are you going?" He apparently heard me calling for a cab. I told him 'Marble Arch'. He said he was going to St. John's Wood or Regent's Park and would drop me on [the] way. I agreed to this. A cab pulled up and we got in. I told the cab driver*

to drop me at Porchester Place. The cab drove off. Whilst I was in the cab with the airman, he said to me, "I should have been in by eleven o'clock," (Regents Park or St. Johns Wood, wherever he was) "could I spend an hour with you? I will give you £2 for a present." I agreed to this. I stopped the cab at Porchester Place near Polygon Mews. We got out of the cab and he paid the driver.

I was dressed either in a dark brown costume or a black one. It is most likely to be the brown one. We walked through Polygon Mews to my flat, which is fifty to sixty yards down on the right, over a lock up garage and situated on the first floor. I unlocked the door and he came up to my flat with me.

Soon after he got in the flat he gave me three £1 notes, they were old notes, by that I mean well used. I put the money on the mantlepiece. I did have a handbag with me. He took his overcoat off and his hat and sat on the side of the bed, in the front bed-sitting room. He was quite normal. I knew he had been drinking because I smelt drink, but he certainly was not drunk and definitely not under the influence of drink. He also told me he had been drinking. He remained with me for over an hour, we were talking all the time. I was about to take off my skirt, which had a zip fastener, when he said, "That won't be necessary, I only want to talk. I have been drinking too much." I sat on a chair on the opposite side of the room.

During the course of conversation he told me he had been in the 'Brassiere Universelle', Piccadilly, where he had left his gas mask. I said to him, "Won't you get in to trouble being out in the street without a gas mask?" He said, "No one will see me at that time of night."

I had a service gas mask in my flat and I said to him, "I have one here you can have," and gave him one. I should like to explain that when I came home from Piccadilly on the previous Saturday night, that would be 7th February 1942, shortly after midnight, I had previously been shopping and to the pictures and had some parcels with me. I took a taxicab from outside the 'Nut House', Regent Street, and drove home to my flat and got out at Porchester Place and Polygon Mews. I picked up my parcels when I left the cab, it was very dark and after I had dismissed the cab I realised I had picked up a service gas mask with my parcels, this must have been left on the seat of the cab. I intended afterwards to hand this to the Police, but for some unknown reason, I forgot to do this.

As has already been stated, the timing of when this statement was taken does not make sense, nor do parts of its contents. Initially, the unnamed woman states that a man believed to be Cummins returned to her flat with her, where they arrived at 2.30 am on Saturday, 13 February, and that Cummins stayed with her for just over an hour before leaving. She also mentions picking up a gasmask from the back of the cab she was in shortly after midnight on the previous Saturday, 7 February. However, the previous Saturday must have been 6 February not 7.

Another discrepancy is that she says she gave the man the gasmask she had picked up from the back of the cab. This means she must either have got her dates wrong, or the man she was with was not Gordon Cummins. Let me explain. On the evening of Saturday, 13 February a young woman called Margaret Heywood was attacked and strangled into unconsciousness by a man in the

Piccadilly Circus area of West London. He was interrupted by an 18-year-old delivery boy by the name of John Swine, and escaped by running off into the night. A gasmask was found in the doorway of the premises where Heywood was attacked, which was not hers, but had been left behind by the man who had attacked her. When further investigated by the police, the gasmask was found to have been allocated to Gordon Cummins. Yet according to the unnamed women who gave the statement, some sixteen hours earlier she had given Cummins a stranger's gasmask because he did not have one with him, which, if correct, should have then been the same one that was left behind at the scene of the attack on Heywood, but it was not.

The statement goes on:

> *Whilst he was with me nothing of an immoral nature took place. He said he wanted to talk to pass an hour away as it would be easier for him to get in at a later hour. He was well spoken. I did mention to him that I was a married woman and had two children. He told me that he was in the Air Force before the war.*
>
> *I am certain that the day I have been speaking about was 13th February 1942, because that was the only night I was down in the Piccadilly area late.*

The following part of her statement is extremely important in so far as it confirms that the man she was talking about was, in fact, Gordon Cummins.

> *I think sometime in March 1942, I was visited by a man who said he was a solicitor, I don't remember his name. He told me*

he was working for a man named Gordon Cummins. I knew he meant a man charged with murder. I had read the papers. He showed me a photograph, head and shoulders, of a man in uniform, and I recognised it as the man I have spoken about in this statement. I told the solicitor exactly what I have said in this statement regarding the time I was with this airman. I also added that what I could say would not do him any good, because he would have had plenty of time to commit a murder in Sussex Gardens, both before I met him and after he left me. I did not make a statement, in writing, to the solicitor, but he said to me, "If the Police get in touch with you let me know." I said to him, "I think I had better go to the 'Yard' at once," and he said, "No, don't do that, your name has not been mentioned and isn't likely to be." I was also visited by the man Cummins' father. He was with the solicitor on one of the two occasions when the solicitor called on me at my flat.

There was another aspect to this statement which never really came to light. The solicitors working on behalf of Cummins were Harold Kenwright & Cox. The obvious questions here are why did they go to such an effort to trace this woman, yet having done so, not obtain a statement from her, nor call her as a witness in the case? Having read through the women's statement it would appear that they had hoped to use her as an alibi to try to show that Cummins could not have murdered Doris Jouannet, because at the time of her death, he was, in fact, with this other woman. The suggestion could easily be made that the only reason Cummins met up with this woman was for no other purpose than to use her as an alibi for himself, knowing that he fully intended to commit a murder later that same night.

Once it became clear to Cummins' solicitors that the woman could not provide the alibi they were hoping for, there would have been no point obtaining a statement from her or calling her as a witness. It would also serve their purpose for the police not to discover the existence of this woman.

Document #40 is an official typed copy of the inquest, which in essence was simply a "rubber stamping" of the formal announcement of when, where and how Gordon Cummins met his death. It took place on 25 June 1942 at Wandsworth Prison before the Coroner for the County of London, Mr Raymond Benedict Hervey Wyatt, and a jury of seven men.

Document #55 concerns the appeal against the death sentence handed down to Gordon Cummins and consists of a typed letter dated 18 June 1942. It is signed by the Chairman, Treasurer and Hon. Secretary of the Looe (Cornwall) Branch of an organisation that in the body of the letter is referred to as, "The People's Common Law Council", although the heading at the top of the page refers to, "The People's Common Law Parliament". Regardless of what their actual title was, they had taken the liberty of writing their letter to the then Home Secretary, the Rt. Hon. Herbert Morrison, at the Home Office in London. It read as follows:

Sir, We, the members of the Council of the Looe Branch of the People's Common Law Council, make this Petition on behalf of Frederick Gordon Cummins, a cadet in the Air Force, who was sentenced for murder. We understand that an appeal was made against this sentence, but was dismissed on the 9th inst.

We are a non-political, non-sectarian body, holding Christian principles, and we feel it is against the teachings of our Master, Jesus Christ, that capital punishment should be inflicted on any man or woman.

We further beg that the fact that this man was serving in the Royal Air Force should be taken in to consideration, as although it may not have been within the province of the medical authorities to find him insane, we feel that the abnormal times in which we are living would have a psychological effect on the mental outlook of many young men serving in the forces, whereby they would tend to hold human life less valuable than in normal times.

We beg for a reprieve against sentence of death upon the above grounds.

Although the letter is asking for a reprieve of the death sentence handed down to Cummins, they cannot even get his name right, calling him Frederick Gordon instead of Gordon Frederick. Rather than try to challenge the sentence with something substantial, as Cummins' legal team had done by claiming falsification and planting of evidence, as well as disputing fingerprint evidence against their client, the best that The People's Common Law Parliament could come up with was the unfounded suggestion that Cummins might in fact be insane. Yet Cummins had never seen active service in the war, so it is unlikely that any post-traumatic stress could have been attributed to this.

Document #57 is the Home Office's response to The People's Common Law Parliament letter and was addressed to the organisation's head office at Woking, Surrey, and dated 23 June 1942.

Sir,

With reference to your petition of the 15th June on behalf of Gordon Frederick Cummins, I am directed by the Secretary of State to inform you that he has given careful consideration to your representations and to all the circumstances of the case, and to express to you his regret that he has failed to discover any sufficient ground to justify him in advising His Majesty to interfere with the due course of the Law.

I am sir
Your obedient servant
F A Newsam

Documents #62 and #63 are a two-page typed letter sent from the editor of the *New Statesman and Nation*, Kingsley Martin. This weekly review of politics and literature held what would certainly be considered "far left" views when it came to politics. Founded in 1913, it had the support of such individuals as the well-known Irish playwright, critic and political activist, George Bernard Shaw.

Kingsley Martin's letter was dated 18 June 1942 and was addressed to Home Secretary Herbert Morrison, personally.

Dear Herbert,

I hope you won't think I'm butting in on something that is not my business if I write to you about the case of Gordon Cummins, who is condemned to death and due to be hanged next Thursday. It happens that I am in close touch with people who know the details, and although I don't pretend to have mastered them myself, I have been convinced that there is a very strong element of doubt in the Cummins' case. I think there is good reason to believe that the Court was influenced by the knowledge that he was also charged with three other murder cases and that the police were probably very anxious to get all these four cases crossed off their books at the same time.

On the face of it I should have thought that Cummins had a good defence against the other charges, and that, therefore, unless these are tried, they ought to have no bearing on the minds of those investigating the case on which he was convicted.

I am a good deal impressed with the fact that a civilian was known to have been with the murdered woman up to ten minutes before the time when Sir Bernard Spilsbury believed that she had been murdered, and it is suggested that it is by no means impossible that this civilian may still turn up.

I am not pretending that I am in a position fully to judge the evidence, but I am convinced that there is an element of doubt, and I should like to feel sure that the points that have made me doubtful were also called to your attention. I know that the responsibility in such cases must be one of the heaviest tasks that a Home Secretary has to shoulder, and I know you well enough to feel sure that you would not wish me to keep silent in a case where I feel that you might inadvertently sanction a gross miscarriage of justice.

I recall a remark of Lord Birkenhead that it was always extremely difficult to persuade a jury to dissociate the shock they got from a particularly horrible crime from the quite different question whether the man before them committed that particular crime.

Yours
Kingsley Martin

The Home Secretary replied to this correspondence in a brief and to the point manner in a one-page typed letter dated 23 June 1942, which is document #61 in Cummins' National Archive file.

> *My dear Kingsley,* [Handwritten]
>   *Thank you for your letter of the 18ᵗʰ about the case of Gordon Frederick Cummins.*
>   *I have carefully and sympathetically considered all the circumstances of this case and the representations which you have made, but I regret that I have failed to discover any grounds which would justify me in advising His Majesty to interfere with the due course of law.*
>
> > *Yours sincerely* [Handwritten]
> > *Herbert Morrison* [Stamped]

Document #80 is particularly interesting. It is a typed letter dated 16 June 1942, just nine days before Cummins was executed at Wandsworth Prison. It was sent by Cummins' solicitors, Harold Kenwright & Cox, who were situated in Wandsworth, their office being not very far from Wandsworth Prison, to the Home Secretary Herbert Morrison. It reads as follows:

> *Sir,*
>   *In reference to our letter to you of yesterday's date, may we draw your attention to recent news reported in the papers concerning a Sgt. Tom Roland Hutchings of the R.A.F. who has been charged in Pennfield, New Brunswick, with the*

murder of a woman, under almost similar conditions to those in this case.

Sgt. Hutchings arrived in Canada from this country just over two months ago, and it is possible that he might have been concerned in the murders with which Cummins was charged.

We have ascertained from the Air Ministry that Sgt. Hutchings was during the period 8th February to the 15th February, stationed at Nuneaton, Warwickshire. According to records he signed out from the Sergeants Mess after lunch on 10th February, returning to breakfast on the 12th February. He might well have been in London on the night when Mrs. Lowe was murdered.

The object of this letter is to ask you to postpone the execution of Cummins until after a copy of the fingerprints of Sgt. Hutchings has been obtained from Canada in order that they can be compared with the fingerprints which the prosecution intended to use in the Lowe case, viz., those of a right-handed man.

Furthermore, we should like an opportunity of making some enquiry into the murder of Mrs, Margaret Rice, the W.A.A.F. Corporal, which bears a strong resemblance to the methods adopted in the murders of which Cummins was accused.

This was clearly a last gasp and desperate attempt by Cummins' defence team to try to gain a stay of execution, whilst at the same time trying to shed sufficient doubt on his conviction and persuade the police to look elsewhere for the 'person responsible for the murder' of Margaret Lowe. Even if Hutchings had killed her, although there has never been any evidence provided to suggest that he did, it still does not answer the question of who killed Hamilton, Oatley and Jouannet, and who attacked Mulcahy and Heywood.

The reference to Hutchings was in relation to the murder of 19-year-old Bernice Connors, who went missing after having attended a dance on the evening of Friday, 25 June 1942 at the community hall in Blacks Harbour, Charlotte County, New Brunswick, Canada.

Connors was seen to leave the dance during the course of the evening in the company of 21-year-old Royal Air Force sergeant Thomas Roland Hutchings. She was never seen alive again. Her parents reported her as missing the following evening, and not long after that a search was begun along her last known route, and her body discovered. A later medical examination revealed that she had been raped.

Hutchings was interviewed in connection with the incident on Sunday, 27 June and stated that he had not murdered Bernice Connors. Despite this he was subsequently arrested and charged with her rape and murder. When the case went to court on 29 September, so many witnesses were produced by the prosecution that it took until 5 October for all their evidence to be heard. The twelve-man jury found Hutchings guilty as charged, but recommended that mercy be shown. The judge in the case, Mr Justice C.D. Richards, ignored the recommendation and sentenced him to death by hanging. The death sentence was carried out at St Andrew's Prison on 16 December 1942, with Hutchings still pleading his innocence. It is a long-held opinion that the evidence against Hutchings was circumstantial at best.

The Margaret Rice referred to in the letter was 24 years of age and a corporal in the WAAF when her dead body was discovered on Saturday, 13 June 1942 in Newcastle-upon-Tyne. She had severe head injuries and was found partly unclothed on a grass verge by the side of the road by a milkman doing his rounds. The injuries were believed to have been caused by a jagged instrument. Margaret was the wife of Lieutenant Patrick Rice, who at the time was serving with the Royal Artillery. A 21-year-old local man, William Ambrose Collins, was arrested and charged with her murder. He was subsequently found guilty and sentenced to death. He was hanged at Durham Gaol on the morning of Wednesday, 28 October 1942, having never been interviewed or seriously suspected of having killed any of the women whom Cummins had been convicted of murdering.

Gordon Cummins' wife, Marjorie, had written in similar terms to the Home Secretary Herbert Morrison, also making reference to the murder of Margaret Rice.

The letters protesting Gordon Cummins' innocence, most of which had ended up on the desk of Herbert Morrison, included those sent by Cummins' sister, Mary Johnson, who was married to a serving lieutenant in the British Army. Other letters included those from his father John Cummins, as well as Mr James Maxton, the Independent Labour Party MP for Bridgeton in Glasgow; Mrs Violet Van-der-Elst, a well-known individual of the time who was a vocal campaigner against capital punishment; the Archbishop of Canterbury; and the Hon. Mrs Randolph Churchill, the Prime Minister's mother, who had written her letter on 10 Downing Street-headed paper.

The letters were written either in disbelief that Cummins was capable of such actions, or claimed that if he *had* committed the murders, then he would have only done so if he were mad. Some letters believed he had not had a fair trial, and some, regardless of whether they believed he was the murderer or not, simply asked for him to be given clemency.

Document #97 is interesting as it is a one-page typed letter from somebody by the name of A. Stanley R. Rundle, a Works Manager from Northampton and a member of the local Society of Friends, who knew Cummins in his teenage years. It is dated 8 May 1942, and although it does not say, it is likely it was sent to the Home Secretary, Herbert Morrison.

I knew Gordon Frederick Cummins personally during his student years in Northampton some eleven or twelve years ago, and even at that time I was well aware of an irregularity in his mental make-up.

I knew him most of the time as a courteous, kindly and generous lad, whereas on occasions he appeared an entirely different person: bitter, selfish and unscrupulous. On these latter occasions, I distinctly remember his very much exaggerated stories of the most brutal treatment he alleged he received at home, and I do feel, as I did then, that such stories could only have been the figment of an abnormal mind.

I would therefore earnestly beg, if Gordon Cummins is found to have been guilty of these horrible crimes, that a very thorough investigation be made into his mental condition and mental history, with a view to receiving appropriate treatment.

A. Stanley R. Rundle

There was no explanation as to how or why the letter was included as part of Cummins' file. One can only assume he had been asked to send the letter to support the theory that Cummins could have been suffering from some kind of mental disorder in the hope it would help him receive clemency. The person most likely to have asked him to send the letter was Cummins' father, who appeared to be leading the attempts to convince the Home Secretary to reprieve his son.

Constance Beach, wife of Major General William Henry Beach CB CMG DSO, a decorated senior army officer, sent a two-page typed letter to the Home Secretary dated 15 June 1942. The letters, documents #114 and #115, are platitudes about Cummins and his family, and read more like a character reference from a family friend.

Acquainted as I am with the family and the upbringing and home influence that the boy has had [Cummins was 28 years of age at the time] *one cannot help feeling that some ghastly mistake has been made. The absence of any incentive or motive for the crime, the "obvious" nature of the clues, the lack of positive proof of his guilt and the fact that there was no mark of any sort on his clothes, all point to it.*

He has always been a devoted son and his wife vouches for the fact that he has been a kind and gentle husband. How can one believe, therefore, that he should suddenly commit a series of murders for no rhyme or reason whatever!

That is what he was suspected of and this fact was known to the Judges of the Court of Appeal as the prosecution referred to it, quite wrongfully, considering that he was TRIED at the Old Bailey for only one of the murder cases, that apparently being the law. This latter point made it impossible for the defending Counsel, Mr Pritt, K.C., to refer to the other cases in which he could have proved an alibi.

The prosecution naturally charged him with the case in which an alibi could not be produced, but as there were the same "obvious" clues in one of the other cases, (the watch found in the respirator that he was carrying which was not his own) it points to the fact that the same culprit laid both sets of clues and should be sought for. Only a madman would steal a watch and a cigarette case and carry them about after murdering their owners. I marvel that this did not occur to the police after an alibi was provided which cleared him completely of one, at least, of the charges of which he was suspected.

It is, in fact, quite normal for some killers, particularly those with psychopathic tendencies, to keep souvenirs or trophies from the bodies or locations of those they have murdered. Some would take personal items such as jewellery, others would take lockets of hair and, in extreme cases, even body parts such as fingers or ears.

The following extract from the letter is both confusing and contradictory at the same time. On the one hand, Mrs Beach says that Cummins was a young man of good character and reputation and inferred that he was an innocent man, but then drifts off in to a "what if" scenario concerning the possibility that he may have committed the murders because of a split personality.

As there is a strong element of doubt of his guilt, which is shared by all who know him and his family, may I urge you to consider the matter of a reprieve for Gordon Cummins on the following grounds. Firstly, for a young man of good reputation to suddenly behave like a fiend or maniac during

*one week only of his life, could only be a case of split personality
or temporary obsession, and should receive medical attention
and surveillance for some considerable time. Secondly, if he
is innocent a certain amount of time should be allowed to
elapse for the real culprit (there is one already suspected by
his father) to be traced and found before the death penalty
deprives a perfectly innocent man of his life.*

One minute Mrs Beach is convinced Cummins is an innocent
man, and the next she is saying that if he was a killer, it was only
because he had a split-personality. It would appear she had no clue
as to whether Cummins was innocent or guilty but, for whatever
reason, she saw fit to involve herself in the case:

*The fact that there are so many grave doubts in this case gives
me the courage to write this letter and ask for your earnest
consideration of the matter of granting a reprieve, even if it
was limited to a period of time for the reasons stated above.*

What is quite amazing in the Cummins case is that so many
individuals from what would be classed as the upper echelons of
British society were prepared and willing to write to the Home
Secretary on his behalf. Although some were at least acquainted
with the family, if not Cummins directly, many of them had no
personal knowledge of Cummins at all or had even met him, but
they were almost queueing up to help him in whatever way they
could. He had certainly become somewhat of a "cause célèbre".

Document #121 and #122 is the hand-written letter sent to
the Home Secretary by Pamela Churchill, the daughter-in-law of
Prime Minister Winston Churchill, written on official 10 Downing
Street paper.

Dear Mr Morrison,

I have received the enclosed rather painful letter, which I would be very grateful if you would read.

I know nothing more of the case, but I am sure that you will see that there has been no miscarriage of justice.

Please forgive me for bothering you.

Pamela Churchill

The letter she was referring to relates to documents #123, #124, #125, #126, and #127, and had been written by Mary Johnson, Cummins' sister. The letter is hand-written in blue ink, is five pages long, and dated 9 June 1942.

The opening paragraph appears to be an attempt at trying to gain empathy with Pamela Churchill, but she soon proceeds to the matter in hand.

Dear Mrs Churchill,

I am writing to you because I feel you would be able to understand my position. I am about your age, and like you, I have a husband serving overseas, but unlike your husband, my husband is a mere Lieutenant.

My very darling eldest brother is Gordon Cummins, the R.A.F cadet who has been sentenced to death for the murder of four women. And today our appeal has failed. My mother and my sister-in-law are heartbroken.

I want to tell you, and I know it to be true, that my brother is completely innocent of these crimes.

This was, of course, nothing more than the words of a desperate woman, at her wits end with nowhere else to turn. After all, she could not possibly know, with any degree of certainty, of her brother's innocence.

The letter continues with Mrs Johnson blaming the inabilities of her brother's legal representative, who had been paid for under the legal aid scheme, to defend him properly, whilst pointing out that the subsequent appeal against conviction could only be based on the content and evidence used in that case.

She continues:

> *But in spite of all these legal proceedings I cannot see why a very brave, fine, innocent man should be hanged for crimes he hasn't done, and knows nothing about whatsoever.*
>
> *Gordon has a wonderful record in the RAF and has done very valuable work. You will realise that if he were guilty of these horrible crimes, his family would hardly fight to the last for him.*

Family members will always want to believe the best of one of their own, and would struggle to admit that one of their nearest and dearest could possibly be a monster. To do so would be a negative reflection on themselves, both collectively and as individuals. Did they miss something? Should they have noticed traits in him that they had not previously seen? The easiest way for them to deal with the situation was to be in denial as that way they need not deal with the obvious truth and evidence that existed against their loved one.

After more words of blind and devoted love for her brother, and a number of reasons as to why he should not be hanged, Mary Johnson ends the letter by asking for Mrs Churchill's help in the matter: 'If you could help just a little we should all be so very grateful'.

Cummins' solicitors, Harold Kenwright & Cox, sent a five-page typed letter addressed to the Home Secretary, dated 15 June 1942. This is covered by documents #159 through to and including #163.

> *Sir,*
>
> *We are acting on behalf of Gordon Frederick Cummins, who is at Wandsworth Prison under sentence of death.*
>
> *On his behalf, and on behalf of his wife and his father and mother, we are making this appeal to you to exercise your prerogative and advise His Majesty to grant a reprieve; and in support thereof we think it right to call your attention to the following facts.*

The letter continues with a number of points of information the Home Secretary was fully aware of. Kenwright reminds the Home Secretary that Cummins was 28 years of age, had been in the RAF for six years and, before his arrest and detention, had been training to become a pilot. He also points out the different times proffered as the time of death for Evelyn Oatley, claiming that the last person seen with her had, in fact, been a civilian who had never been traced. Where Kenwright acquired the information that the last person seen with Evelyn Oatley had been dressed in civilian clothes is unclear, as information provided from an unnamed neighbour had stated the man in question had, in fact, been in RAF uniform.

Kenwright then brings up the issue of a lack of blood being discovered on Cummins or any of his clothing, something that he says would have been expected in such a murder case. The reason why no such blood was ever discovered had been covered in a report submitted by Detective Chief Inspector Edward Greeno, which explained how, because she had been strangled to near death, and certainly into unconsciousness, the blood flow in her body was circulating at a much slower pace, meaning there was no spurting of blood from the wounds inflicted on her body.

Kenwright then raises the issue of a cigarette case which had been found inside a fridge in the kitchenette area at Cummins' billet, pointing out that there was no actual forensic or visual evidence which proved beyond all reasonable doubt that Cummins was the individual who placed it there. On this matter, Kenwright makes a good point. The kitchenette was a communal area and any number of RAF pilot cadets had access to it at any given time, which also means that any one of those same individuals could have also placed the cigarette case in the fridge. Nevertheless, Cummins was the only suspect the police looked for in connection to the murder of Evelyn Oatley.

The next point raised is that of the two fingerprints found on items at Oatley's flat. Despite the renowned fingerprint expert Cherrill's statement that both fingerprints were a match with Cummins' prints, Kenwright does not feel that Cherrill's evidence alone was sufficient to condemn their man to the gallows, even though he provides no further explanation as to why this was so.

In relation to Margaret Lowe, who was murdered sometime during the evening of 10 February and the early hours of 11 February, Kenwright's submission is that Cummins was in his billet at 11 pm, having decided not to go out that evening, and that there was no evidence to prove he had gone out after that hour. In highlighting this Kenright conveniently forgets to point out that it was common practice between the airmen to sign in and out for each other, or to record a convenient time for their arrival/departure, which may not always have been accurate.

For the murder of Doris Jouannet, Kenwright goes into some detail to make his point, which in essence is that at the time she was murdered, Cummins was probably, although not definitely, in the company of another woman, and had been for two hours. This being the case, Kenwright said, Cummins could not have murdered Doris Jouannet. It was also the same night that both Margaret Heywood and Catherine Mulcahy were attacked.

> *We have succeeded in tracing the woman (who is referred to as "the woman in black") and her name and address can be disclosed by us if necessary. Cummins went with her in a taxi–cab from Piccadilly Circus to her flat which is a mews as described by Cummins who spent nearly two hours with her before returning to his billet at St. James Close. This stay with the woman was probably at the time when Mrs Jouannet was murdered, and if it be so, Cummins could not have been the murderer.*

When it comes to the murder of Evelyn Hamilton, the first of the four women to be killed, Kenwright claims that there was no evidence to prove that a pencil belonging to her, and found in a dustbin at Cummins' billet, was placed there by him. Kenwright's suggestion is that it could just as easily have been planted there by somebody else, possibly the man who had murdered Hamilton. On closer examination his words appear somewhat devoid of any real substance. Why would somebody go to the extremes of brutally murdering four women, and attacking two more, and then try to frame Cummins? In any case, for the murder of Oatley, the only one which Cummins was subsequently charged with, the police had fingerprint evidence recovered from the crime scene, which was a direct match with his.

He also raises the matter of the mortar dust from the floor of the air raid shelter where Evelyn Hamilton's body was discovered, and the fact that the same dust was discovered in Cummins' gasmask bag. Kenwright offers no explanation here, simply observing that, 'no one can explain how it could have got there'. This conveniently ignored the obvious answer, that the reason the mortar powder was discovered in Cummins' respirator bag was because he had it with him when he murdered Evelyn Hamilton.

Kenwright then proceeds to offer a character study of Cummins. Although it begins sensibly enough, it goes on to say something any individual facing a death sentence would not want their solicitor to say on their behalf.

> *In the words of Mr Justice Asquith, the murder of Mrs Oatley was a "sadistic sexual murder of a ghoulish and horrible type". This would also describe the Murders of Mrs Lowe and Mrs Jouannet, and the murder of Miss Hamilton might also come under the same category. Cummins is not a sadist, and apart from his connection with [name redacted] and "the woman in black" there is no evidence of sexual desires. His wife gives him a good character in every respect, and in her own words, "he would not hurt a fly". This bears out Cummins' positive statement that he is completely innocent.*
>
> *But if he did commit the crimes he must at the time have been suffering from [a] split mind and is not accountable for his actions.*

This statement was not exactly helpful to Cummins' claim that he was innocent of all charges against him. By allowing such an admission to be connected to his name, all Kenwright has done is to sow the seed of doubt into the Home Secretary's mind as to Cummins' innocence.

Near to the end of his letter, Kenwright talks of two other murders and an attempted murder made during the same week Cummins murdered Evelyn Oatley. However, he is not clear about whether these were Doris Jouannet, Margaret Lowe and Margaret Heywood, or three totally different women.

In closing his letter, Kenwright makes two very good points. The Lord Chief Justice had said that the trial judge, Justice Asquith, may well have read the depositions about the murders of the three other women, all of which Cummins had been charged with. If this was the case, he may have had this in his mind when summing up to the jury. Kenwright also points out that the three judges who heard Cummins' appeal were also more than likely to have known of the other murders he had initially been charged with, even though he was only eventually on trial for the murder of Evelyn Oatley, meaning that they were biased when they took the decision to dismiss his appeal.

Kenwright ends his letter by saying, 'It is for these reasons that Cummins now appeals for clemency, and asks you to advise His Majesty to exercise his prerogative and grant a reprieve.'

Document #213 is another of the letters sent to the Home Secretary pleading for clemency on behalf of Cummins. It was sent by the Bishop of Guildford, John Victor Macmillan OBE, who was also the uncle of Harold Macmillan, the future British Prime Minister. It was dated 10 July 1942.

Dear Mr. Morrison,

I write this letter with some hesitation. It is about the case of a man called Cummins who has been sentenced to death for murder, whose parents live at Woking, their address is Mr. and Mrs. Cummins, Uplands, Maybury, Woking.

It would obviously be entirely out of place if I was to say anything at all about the case itself: I know nothing of the facts. I have, however, been impressed by what the Rural Dean of Woking, who is a very sensible and experienced man, tells me about the father and mother. They are in charge of a Remand Home there and have given an account of the son up to the time when he went in to the R.A.F. as having borne a good character.

I understand that a petition has been sent in asking if the prerogative of mercy could be extended in this case and as the parents wrote to me and I know from the Rural Dean of Woking that they are themselves, good people, I felt I ought perhaps to send a line to add to the plea for mercy if it can be rightly considered. I do so on behalf of the parents.

Yours sincerely
John Macmillan

It is quite startling to consider that such a learned man of the cloth, and one who held such high position within the church, should be more than willing to make a plea for mercy on behalf of a man who he did not know, had never met, and had been convicted of the brutal murder of a defenceless woman. Macmillan's plea for clemency on behalf of Cummins could be interpreted in two ways.

It could be that it had a singular purpose, to try to save Cummins' life because he believed him to be innocent of the crimes he was accused of, or it could be that he was asking for clemency in relation to his death sentence. Unfortunately, Macmillan's letter does not make it clear which he is advocating for. Either way, it was an attempt to save Cummins' life. He claims to have known nothing of the facts of the case, which is highly unlikely given the press coverage at the time, and also fails to make a single reference to any of the four women believed to have been murdered by Cummins.

However, the contents of the letter are not what makes the bishop's attempt at influencing the case in Cummins' favour incredulous, but rather the fact that it is dated 10 July, fifteen days after Cummins was executed at Wandsworth Prison. Why would somebody do that? The bishop was obviously an intelligent man and Cummins' execution would have been a national news item. It would not have been something he would have easily missed. The only logical explanation appears to be that the date on the letter was typed incorrectly. Anything else simply does not make any sense.

An example of the widespread reporting of Gordon Cummins and the murders he was suspected of having committed came in the form of an article in *The Star* newspaper dated 17 February 1942, the same day he appeared at Bow Street Police Court charged with the murders of Evelyn Oatley, Margaret Lowe and Doris Jouannet.

The Star was an extremely popular newspaper, especially amongst Londoners, with demand often being more than the available supply. In the years immediately after the end of the Second World War, readership of the paper was more than 1 million, and on 20 November 1947, the day of the marriage between Princess

Elizabeth and Prince Philip, the paper sold a staggering 1,414,660 copies.

A cutting from this article of 17 February forms document #217.

R.A.F. MAN IN COURT: 3 MURDER CHARGES

Gordon Frederick Cummins, a 28-year-old R.A.F. aircraftsman, appeared at Bow-street today, charged with the murder of three women in the West End of London, and was remanded until Friday. The women are:

*Mrs. **Evelyn Oatley**, also known as Leta Ward, 30, a blonde, found stabbed in her Wardour-street, Soho, flat last Tuesday;*

*Mrs. **Margaret Florence Lowe**, 43, a brunette, found strangled in her flat at Gosfield-street, W., on Friday; and*

*Mrs. **Doris Jouannet**, 32, wife of a London hotel manager, discovered strangled in bed at Sussex-gardens, Paddington, also on Friday.*

A small crowd gathered outside the police buildings an hour before the opening of the court.

Among the onlookers were several women who shouted when a police car containing Cummins was driven in to the yard of the court buildings.

The blinds of the car were drawn and they did not catch a glimpse of him.

The crowd increased as the time for the opening of the court drew near. A number of women, some of them very well dressed, were among the public admitted.

Cummins, who was described as an aircraftsman, is rather a slight man, of soldierly build, fresh complexioned, and with dark hair brushed back from his forehead.

> *When Chief Inspector Edward Greeno, of Scotland Yard,*
> *entered the witness box, Cummins sat and gazed straight in*
> *front of him. He did not once glance around the court.*
>
> *Chief Inspector Greeno said that about 10 a.m. today,*
> *at the rear of the court, he charged Cummins with the three*
> *murders. When cautioned he made no reply.*
>
> *Remanding Cummins until Friday, the Magistrate (Mr.*
> *H. McKenna) said that he was already due to appear before*
> *him on another charge.*
>
> *When asked if he had anything to say before being*
> *remanded, Cummins whispered, "No, sir," so quietly that he*
> *could hardly be heard.*
>
> *Cummins, who wore an R.A.F. greatcoat over his tunic,*
> *stood at attention when remanded, and then walked smartly*
> *out of court.*
>
> *Among about 30 people who waited outside were a few*
> *R.A.F. men.*

The article appeared just two months before Cummins' Old
Bailey trial at which he was found guilty and sentenced to
death. After the glut of similar newspaper articles reporting the
atrocities he had allegedly carried out, there would have been
few people who had not either read or heard about the number
of murders he had originally been charged with, including those
people who were eventually selected to sit on the jury. This, of
course, begs the question as to how Cummins could ever have
received a fair trial.

Document #218 is also a newspaper cutting. This one is
from the *News of the World* dated 28 June 1942, three days after
Cummins was executed.

'RIPPER' PAYS THE LAST PENALTY

London's modern "Jack the Ripper," 28-year-old R.A.F. cadet, Gordon Frederick Cummins, has paid the price for atrocities which shocked and startled the country.

He was executed at Wandsworth Gaol, and went unflinchingly to the scaffold.

Although there was overwhelming evidence that Cummins committed at least four murders, there is one woman who will never believe in his guilt.

She is his wife, secretary to a famous London theatre manager, who told a News of the World *reporter yesterday:-*

"I know the world believes him guilty, but until I die I will never believe he was capable of the revolting murders for which he has been hanged. I believe in his innocence."

Cummins, who died because of his over weaning vanity, was one of the strangest murderers ever to be tried at the Old Bailey.

For many years it will be debated in legal and police circles whether this maniacal killer was sane or insane.

Theorists will point to "split-mind" and other mental causes for his killings, but detectives who had most to do with the investigation, and with his arrest, are satisfied that Cummins was one of the sanest men who ever stood in a dock while a judge passed sentence of death.

They believe Cummins argued in his mind the whole problem before he committed his first murder. They believe he said to himself: "Having decided to murder to obtain money, I am satisfied that if I introduce revolting details in the treatment of the bodies of my victims, the police will be convinced that a madman was responsible. As I am absolutely sane, and as the police will be looking for a madman, they cannot possibly suspect me."

But Cummins had not counted on the ingenuity of Chief-Insp E Greeno of Scotland Yard, and in the generally accepted fact that a murderer always makes one mistake.

Like most of his kind, Cummins made the mistake. In a struggle with a woman in London's Haymarket, a woman no doubt marked down as another of his victims, Cummins was interrupted, as he strove to strangle her, by a small boy, who flashed a torch. In his haste to get away Cummins dropped his gas-mask, and on the case was his regimental number.

The woman referred to in the article was clearly Margaret Heywood, whilst the "small boy" was 18-year-old John Shine.

POLICE PROOF
Within a matter of hours Cummins had been arrested on a charge of assault. Very soon he was charged with three murders.

All three had been revoltingly mutilated, and in each case a left-handed man was responsible, Cummins was left-handed.

There is ample proof that he also murdered Miss Evelyn Hamilton, a 40-year-old chemist, and a woman of irreproachable character, who was found murdered in a Marylebone air-raid shelter.

In each of these four cases complete proof is in the possession of the police, and there is a strong suspicion also that Cummins may have been the murderer of 19-year-old

Mable Church, found strangled and criminally assaulted in Hampstead.

With such detailed information about Cummins plastered all over the newspapers, it certainly did not portray him in a positive way, in fact it could be said, quite the opposite. The Press at the time did not necessarily report on the case in an unbiased manner. By way of example, in the article's last paragraph the author states, 'In each of these cases complete proof is in possession of the police', which was clearly not true. Cummins was only prosecuted for the murder of Evelyn Oatley because the evidence against him in her murder was backed up by fingerprint evidence recovered from the crime scene, which was a direct match to Cummins' own prints. He was not on trial for the other three murders because it was felt that the evidence in each of those cases was not as watertight. If Cummins were ever to receive a posthumous pardon, and there is no suggestion that such a scenario would ever arise, newspaper articles such as this would most definitely not help his cause.

Documents #238 through to #249 make up a twelve-page typed and detailed report submitted by Detective Chief Inspector Edward Greeno to his Superintendent, outlining the entire case against Cummins.

The report begins with Cummins' conviction for the murder of Evelyn Oatley at the Central Criminal Court of the Old Bailey on 28 April 1942, before Mr Justice Asquith, and continues with the dismissal of his appeal against conviction at the Court of Criminal Appeal on 9 June, heard before the Lord Chief Justice, Viscount Caldecote, Mr Justice Humphreys and Mr Justice Tucker.

Greeno's report includes the fact that after Cummins had been found guilty of Evelyn Oatley's murder and sentenced to death, the Home Office had received three appeals against his sentence: one from his solicitors, Messrs Harold Kenwright & Cox: one from his father, John Cummins: and another from his wife, Marjorie Cummins. These three appeals, not surprisingly in the circumstances, contained very similar information. By way of example, they all included the fact that at Cummins' original trial, Sir Bernard Spilsbury had given evidence that the most probable time of Evelyn Oatley's death was 12.30 am on 10 February. In this case, their collective argument was that Cummins' movements on the day in question had, in fact, been accounted for up to and including 12.40 am.

Greeno counters this with evidence obtained from a woman whose name has been partly redacted in the report, but appears to have had the surname of Alyes or Alves, and who was more than likely working as a prostitute at the time. She told the police that she had met up with a man she subsequently discovered was Cummins in the West End, but that they had parted company in Piccadilly Circus at approximately midnight on 9 February. However, she then saw him again in passing at about 12.40 am on 10 February. The point Greeno is making here is that there was no concrete evidence to account for Cummins' whereabouts between the two times the woman had said she had seen him, meaning that he (potentially) had time to meet up with Evelyn Oatley, murder her and then get himself back to the West End by 12.40.

Although this woman was not called as a witness by the prosecution, she was interviewed by police on 20 February and a statement was taken giving her account of her meeting with Cummins on the evening of 9–10 February. She included the fact that she and another woman had met Cummins and a second airman by the name of Johnson, the latter of which she had gone home with.

Greeno's report also includes an explanation about why there would have possibly been a lack of blood on Cummins' person, as well as a lack of blood spurts at Oatley's flat. He refers to Sir Bernard Spilsbury's evidence in relation to Oatley, which was that because Cummins had strangled her into a state of unconsciousness before severing the main vein on the right side of her neck, there would have been no blood spurt. Instead, the blood had "drained" out of the wound, over the side of the divan where her head was laying, and on to the floor where it had gathered.

The other reason for no blood splattering to have been found on Cummins' clothing was a simple one: the chances are that at the time he cut the vein in the side of her neck, both he and Oatley were more than likely naked.

A subsequent search of Cummins' clothing, did, however, reveal two human blood stains, each about an inch long, situated on the inner surface of the belt of his uniform tunic worn at the time of his arrest. One stain was towards the front of the belt and the other around the midline at the back. Although the Director of Public Prosecutions was informed of these discoveries by the police, he determined, somewhat surprisingly, that no useful purpose would be served tendering it as evidence; a decision that is extremely difficult to understand. The only sensible rationale as to why this decision was taken was that the blood stains were discovered three days after the murder had taken place and were already dry. It was therefore believed to be impossible to ascertain with any degree of certainty as to how old the blood was and who it belonged to (DNA testing from blood only became possible in 1985).

Greeno noted that the prosecution had inferred a cigarette case found in the refrigerator at Cummins' billet had been "planted" there by the police. This was based on the fact it was only discovered four days after he had been arrested for the assault on Margaret Heywood, although in Greeno's report, her name has been redacted.

An interesting point of disagreement between the Metropolitan Police and the Royal Air Force arose concerning what had been done with Cummins on his return to his billet. Detective Inspector Jeffrey, of West End Central Police Station, stated that he had contacted the Royal Air Force Police by telephone and asked them to inform him when Cummins returned to his billet as he wished to interview him in relation to his gasmask having been discovered at the scene of the assault on Margaret Heywood. Jeffrey added that he had requested Cummins be detained on his return to the billet, but the Corporal of the Guard and an Orderly Sergeant at the billets stated that no such request had been made.

When Cummins returned to his billet at 4.30 am on 13 February, he was detained by the guard and told by the Orderly Sergeant, Corporal Johnson, that his gasmask had been found at the scene of an assault on a woman near Piccadilly Circus, and that he was to wait in his room until civilian police officers arrived to interview him. This was all well and good, but it was also a big mistake because Corporal Johnson did not physically restrain, search, or detain Cummins so that he could be watched and observed at all times. Instead, Cummins was allowed to go and remain in his room on his own, giving him both the time and opportunity to hide or discard any potential evidence linking him to the offence anywhere in the billet, including any communal areas.

Johnson contacted West End Central Police Station soon after Cummins returned to his billet, and Detective Bennett, accompanied by Constable Sullivan, made his way to Flat 27, St. James' Close, where they arrived at about 5.45 am. Cummins was brought from his room and handed over to Detective Bennett, who informed him that he was taking him to West End Central Police Station to interview him in relation to the attack and assault of Margaret Heywood. What is both surprising and somewhat shocking is that not only did Bennett and Sullivan not search Cummins' room, they did not even visit it. There is no record as to why they failed to do either.

When he arrived at the police station, Cummins was searched and the following items, deemed to be relevant to the case, were found in his possession:

- A piece of paper with Heywood's telephone number on it, which she had given to him earlier in the evening.
- A silver-coloured cigarette case which was later identified by the daughter of Margaret Lowe as being "exactly similar" to one owned by her mother, whose body she had discovered at Flat number 4, 9/10 Gosfield Street.
- A greenish coloured comb which was identified as being the property of Doris Jouannet, who had been found murdered at her flat at 187 Sussex Gardens.
- A service respirator, which contained eight £1 notes and a wristlet watch, the latter of which was subsequently identified as belonging to Doris Jouannet.

At the time of being interviewed in connection with the attack on Margaret Heywod, the officers who dealt with Cummins did not connect him with the murder of Evelyn Oatley, or with any of the murders he was later charged with.

Whilst making further enquiries regarding the attack on Margaret Heywood, detectives from West End Central Police Station, namely Detective Sergeant Crawford and Detective Sergeant Shepherd, visited Cummins' billet at St. James' Close on the evening of 14 February, where they interviewed a number of other Royal Air Force personnel who were staying there. Whilst there, Crawford and Shepherd were shown the room in Flat 27 where Cummins slept and examined his military kit, which was on his bunk. During this search, Sergeant Crawford discovered a fountain pen, inscribed with the letters D and J, in Cummins' spare tunic, but neither he nor Shepherd appreciated its true significance at that time, nor did they conduct a thorough search of the room. The main reason behind this was because they were not there as part of a murder enquiry, but for the assault on Margaret Heywood. The inscription on the pen was not spotted until the following day, when it was then believed to be the same one owned by Doris Jouannet.

The next day, 15 February, Chief Inspector Greeno began reviewing all the information which had so far been obtained by his colleagues relating to the murders of Margaret Lowe and Doris Jouannet. He also looked through the items recovered from Cummins' person and his billet at St. James' Close. He noticed that the fountain pen had the initials DJ engraved on it, and the discovery led him to make contact with Henri Jouannet, the husband of Doris Jouannet, and ask him to attend Marylebone Lane Police Station to view some items of property. He was able to confirm that the fountain pen, found by Detective Sergeant Crawford in a pocket of Cummins' tunic at his billet, and the green comb and wristlet watch, which had been found in his possession when he had been arrested, were all items belonging to his deceased wife, Doris. This information immediately made Cummins a prime suspect in her murder.

Greeno checked with Crawford and Shepherd and discovered that when they went to Cummins' billet on 14 February, they had not carried out a thorough search of his room. Greeno immediately sent Crawford and other officers back to St. James' Close to conduct a search. There had obviously been a breakdown in communication between Greeno and Crawford, or a lack of understanding of what was wanted, because although Crawford and his men thoroughly searched the room where Cummins slept, along with his personal items, they did not search any of the other rooms in the property, which included the kitchenette area.

On the afternoon of 17 February, Greeno telephoned Group Captain Gilligan, the officer in command of the training flight to which Cummins was attached. During this conversation, Gilligan informed Greeno that his men had found a cigarette case and a green-coloured propelling pencil whilst searching the billet themselves, but as he had not placed any real significance on these items, he had not made any previous mention of them.

Despite knowing that both, or either, of these items could be of significant value to his investigation, Greeno did not attend St. James' Close until the afternoon of the following day. His reason for not doing so was down to the fact that he was "otherwise engaged". While accepting he was a busy man, it is hard to understand why, on being informed about the cigarette case and the pencil, he did not immediately dispatch one of his men to go collect them.

Gilligan's comments to Greeno during their telephone conversation are difficult to fathom. The cigarette case, subsequently discovered to belong to Evelyn Oatley, was found by one of his men, Sergeant Moon, in the fridge of the kitchenette at Flat 27, which is hardly the usual location somebody would leave such an item. Meanwhile, Corporal Freeman had found a green propelling pencil, together with a note pad bearing Cummins' name, in the dustbin of the same kitchenette. The pencil was identified as having belonged to Evelyn Hamilton. It was only after this time that a thorough search of Flat 27 was carried out. During this search, Greeno's men found a handkerchief bearing the laundry mark of Evelyn Hamilton, and a pair of rubber soles which had been cut from Cummins' RAF-issued boots. It is hard to believe that anybody other than Cummins would have done this and the only plausible reason for doing so was because he had concerns that he may have left footprints at one of the crime scenes.

Greeno's report mentions the defence's concerns over the reliability of the positive fingerprint identification which connected Cummins to the tin opener and the piece of glass from a makeup mirror, which had been recovered from the scene of Evelyn Oatley's murder. He claims the fingerprint aspect of the case had been dealt with by Superintendent Cherrill, who not only had an impeccable reputation, but was universally accepted as being the foremost fingerprint expert in the world. He stated without any hesitation that the fingerprints found on the tin opener belonged to Cummins, specifically from the little finger of his left hand, whilst the print found on the piece of mirror from the makeup case was from his left thumb. Only four marks of distinction were required on a fingerprint to prove an individual's identity. In this case Cherrill discovered sixteen marks of identification relative to the print found on the tin opener, whilst twenty-five similarities were found in relation to the other fingerprint.

The report also covers the attack on Catherine Mulcahy, although her name is redacted. Greeno states Cummins was unarguably the man responsible for attacking and attempting to strangle her, because two of the £1 notes he gave her bore the serial numbers M.87.D 397808 and M.97.D 397809, which it was later confirmed were given to Cummins as part of his RAF pay he had received the same day he attacked Mulcahy.

In relation to the murder of Margaret Hamilton, whose body was found in the air raid shelter, Greeno claims Cummins was directly connected to this crime by virtue of the fact that pieces of mortar from the inside brickwork of the shelter were found in his gasmask case, samples of which had been taken from the crime scene by Inspector Clare, who had attended the incident. The defence's response to this was to question why such samples were taken and then allege the reason pieces of mortar were found in Cummins' gasmask case was because they had been planted there by the police.

In closing, the report mentions the petitions submitted by members of Cummins' family, as well as his solicitors. It also includes apparent attempts by the defence to delay and defer Cummins' execution by bringing into the equation the murders of two women by other RAF personnel, although one of these murders had taken place in Newcastle, whilst the other had taken place in Canada. The defence wanted the fingerprints of the two men concerned to be checked against those found at the murder scenes of Evelyn Oatley and Margaret Lowe, despite the fact that the prints found at both locations had been positively identified as belonging to Cummins.

Document #263 is a typed letter sent by the Senior Medical Officer at Brixton Prison, where Cummins was being held before his trial. It is dated 13 April 1942 and was sent to the Director of Public Prosecutions.

> *Sir,*
>
> *I have the honour to report as follows regarding the state of mind of the above named* [Gordon Frederick Cummins]:
>
> *He was received here on 17.2.1942 since when he has been under continuous observation in hospital. I have interviewed him, received reports from officers concerning him and have studied the depositions. His father, mother and wife have been interviewed.*
>
> *According to his father there is no history of insanity in the family, nor has his son ever shown any evidence of mental disorder. He adds that his son has always been a normal person and "without any cruelty in his nature".*
>
> *Throughout the period he has been under my care here the accused has been normal in his conduct and rational in conversation. At no time has he exhibited any evidence of mental disease. Though apparently of unemotional type he has not exhibited any lack of interest at interviews. He denies any loss of memory or blackouts at any time in his life.*
>
> *He states he was a moderate drinker until he joined the Royal Air Force in 1935, but since this he has drunk more heavily. He alleges he was drunk on the evenings of the 9th and 12th February.*
>
> *The evidence of Sir Bernard Spilsbury as to the character and sites of the wounds inflicted on the victims points to a sadistic basis for the murders. I have discussed with the accused his sexual life and have only elicited denials of any perversion or deviation from the normal.*

In conclusion I am of the opinion that the accused is sane and fit to plead to the indictment.

Interestingly enough, when the matter was heard in court, no medical evidence was called for or given. It is unclear how and when the question of Cummins' sanity became an issue. I believe it is simply a matter of the prosecution wanting to make sure that their case against Cummins was watertight. By addressing this subject head on, it stopped his defence from claiming he was not in his right mind at the time he committed the murders which, if accepted by the jury, would have more than likely saved him from execution.

There is, of course, another consideration which deserves some discussion. Four women had been brutally murdered and somebody had to pay. Society was aghast that anybody could commit such horrendous crimes. In such circumstances, it is always easier for everybody to accept and understand the situation if the perpetrator was a lunatic or insane. From the government's perspective there are slightly different aspects to consider, albeit the principle of finding the person responsible remains. They were in the middle of fighting a war that would determine a future of either freedom or servitude, making it a war that they simply had to win. One aspect of ensuring a victory was to keep public morale high, which would have been harder to achieve with the population believing there was a mad man on the loose going around killing women at will, and who the authorities were unable to catch.

Very early on the authorities in question had decided that the same person, Cummins, had committed all four murders. There was no consideration that it could have been more than one person, or if there was, they kept it to themselves because it did not suit their narrative. From a public perspective, it would ease their concerns if just one "mad man" had committed the murders. With Cummins convicted of murder and executed, the "bogeyman" was no more, and the nation's population could once again sleep easier in their beds, and public morale, along with confidence in the government, would be restored, and everybody could get back to focusing their thoughts on the war.

Chapter Eight

Family Letters

The National Archives' file on the Cummins case includes a selection of interesting letters written by a variety of people, including Gordon Cummins, his wife Marjorie and his father John. This chapter focuses purely on those letters from family and close friends, the people who knew him intimately, rather than those who, for different reasons, had put pen to paper in attempts to gain him clemency based on nothing more than good intentions.

Some of the correspondence is included here in its entirety, whereas others, which are rather long and quite detailed, are only represented by relevant sections repeated amongst these pages. For ease of reference, the letters are shown here in (roughly) chronological order.

Several of the documents include letters written between Cummins and his wife, Marjorie. Documents #273 and #274 relate to a typed two-page letter he wrote from Wandsworth Prison. It is dated 2 May and shows the close relationship between the couple.

My Darling Marjorie,
Your visit has given me renewed hope and courage and I love you more than ever. Darling, this gross injustice cannot be allowed to stand. Something must be done. It is dreadful to sit here just waiting, knowing full well that I am

*completely innocent of the whole affair. I have been foolish,
but never a murderer.*

*You are very brave, my sweet, and I am very proud of
you; have no fear, everything will work out alright in the
end, I hope.*

*I'd like to know who the devil told the newspapers of our
little joke, the Earl of Buchan, etc. It's not much use pointing
out to people now my peculiar sense of humour.*

Wednesday.

*Three letters have just arrived, one from Mary, one
from mother, and yours. They give me great comfort; it is
comforting to know that there are some who believe me.*

*I am treated here with every consideration; there is a
greater degree of comfort than at Brixton, and that's saying
something! I have plenty of good books from the prison
library, cards, dominoes, draughts, etc, and an issue of 15
cigarettes a day. My food is better, I think, than any I have
tasted in the R.A.F.*

*Of course it is very difficult to settle down quietly under
the present circumstances, as there is always at the back
of my mind the distressing thought that my appeal may
fail! In that event, the person to see would be the Home
Secretary himself. For I have an objection to being punished
for something I haven't done, and I hate to think that the
guilty man remains unpunished. It would be no use dragging
a confession from him if I were one of the minor angels!*

*I do not wear night clothes when being visited, mother.
The neat and fashionable garb in which I was nearly lost
is a prison suit; which garments have been worn by all the
best people from time to time. A great friend of mine, in*

Brixton, first cousin to a well-known Peer, took a pride in these clothes.

I'm rather tired, so I think I'll pop in to bed. Don't forget Saturday, or before then!

All my love,
   Gordon

Continuing the theme of showing the nature of the relationship between Cummins and his wife, Document #177 is a one-page typed letter sent by Marjorie to her husband at Wandsworth Prison. It is not dated, but must have been written before 9 June as on receipt of it, the prison governor wrote to the Home Secretary advising him of its arrival, and that letter is dated 9 June.

Gordon, my dearest love,

Although in a few hours I shall be with you, I feel I want to write so that you will receive a few lines from me on Monday morning before the appeal begins.

I want you to know that nothing can alter my feelings for you and that come what may I shall always believe you innocent. Don't think that I say this because I am pessimistic about the appeal, far from it, but I feel we have to be prepared for anything and I should hate you to think the appeal will influence my thoughts at all. I'm afraid even if we win you will be in for more time, as the public prosecutor is going on with other cases, but don't despair darling. Whatever happens we will go on fighting against injustice and I am sure Mr. Pritt will fight hard too.

I shall be at the court on Monday praying that justice may come. I hope my presence there may help you a bit. I love you so very much it breaks my heart that you should suffer so. Please pray darling and trust in God. We cannot say why this has happened to us, but there must be some purpose in it. There is no need for me to tell you to be brave, for you have been wonderful all through the difficult time and you have our admiration as well as our love. I'm sure men have been awarded the V.C. for going through less than you have endured.

You are in my thoughts night and day darling. You cannot know how much you mean to me and how much I love you. Never was a woman's love greater.

I cannot write more now as I have to get off to work. Good luck darling and God bless you. Every scrap of my love and millions of kisses.

From your adoring wife,
  MARJORIE

This is a letter clearly written by a woman, and devoted wife, who not only loved her husband very much, but who also believed in his absolute innocence. Whether this was because of her interpretation of the facts in the case, because she was totally besotted with the man she loved, or both, is unclear.

It was not only his wife who sent supportive letters. Document #174 is a one-page typed letter written to Cummins by his sister, Mary Johnson, and is dated Tuesday, 9 June.

My Darling Gordon,
  After the farce this morning one doesn't quite know what to say. I am now being very rude to those people who say the court of appeal is fair. I wonder if you noticed Mrs. Goodchild

next to me? She is the Duke of Wellington's great grandniece and is a Wellesley. She was almost speechless with disgust at the Judges. We are all getting hard to work this evening. Please don't think for one moment that we are sitting back now. Marjorie has been furiously pounding away on Daddy's typewriter and we all seem to be whipped in to action.

We were so very proud of you Gordon dear. Your bearing was simply wonderful and I was so glad that you did not let any emotion cross your face in front of the common people. I think Marjorie will be able to tell you all full details when she sees you. Why it should happen to you of all people I don't know, and I think they ought to put Humphries [sic] in your place because they could just as easily prove it on him. He seemed as though he was out to smash the case because the other two judges were all for you heartily until Humphries [sic] started to influence them.

We all came straight home. We cabled John and I do hope he replies, but of course he may be on his way over. I really think that that is why we haven't heard from him for such a long time.

So very many people send their love to you. You have a tremendous backing, you know. I don't think half the people in the court today knew the meaning of the word "Gentleman". And yet our country seems to be in the hands of such people. Why God allows it beats me.

Gordon darling please don't forget that the family and all of our friends and all who know you believe in you absolutely and completely.

Such lots of love
  Mary

This letter is another example of how completely convinced Cummins' family were of his innocence. This despite clear evidence directly connecting him to all the crimes. Cummins was a charming and enigmatic individual, of that there was no doubt, but it is puzzling that everyone in his family was completely convinced he was an innocent man. Whether this was because they were taken in and were loyal to him regardless of the amount of evidence against him, or simply did not want to admit to themselves that one of their own was a monster, which in turn might reflect badly on them, is unclear.

Marjorie Cummins sent a three-page typed letter (documents #251, #252 and #253) to the Home Secretary dated 9 June, the same day Cummins' appeal against his sentence was heard and dismissed by the Lord Chief Justice. She begins with providing a character reference for her husband:

First, I should like to tell you that I have been married to Gordon Cummins for nearly six years, during which time we have been very, very happy, and he has never been anything but kind and tolerant in every respect. He is cultured and well-spoken and has an excellent record of six and a half years' service in the R.A.F.

He is a normal man and is certainly not a sex maniac or a pervert, and medical examination by a doctor of some distinction bears out this fact.

It was not his habit to consort with other women, but during the week in question he twice went out with other members of the R.A.F. and getting very drunk, did as the others did, and picked up prostitutes. I should like to add that although he was not a habitual drunkard, he occasionally went on a real 'binge' and whenever he had too much to

drink he was the reverse of being murderous, in fact he just
passed out quietly for an hour or so.

Despite her efforts, it would appear that although it was clearly not her intention, Mrs Cummins confirms to the Home Secretary that her husband was both a regular heavy drinker and a womaniser. She appears to be amazingly calm and understanding about her husband's sexual dalliances with prostitutes, especially as she had gone out of her way to emphasise how they had been 'very, very happy' during their nearly six years of marriage.

She continues to say that:

I am not writing this just because I am the man's wife, but
because I have studied the case in every detail (including
the fingerprints) ever since my husband was charged on 17ᵗʰ
February, and I can assure you that if I had any doubts
whatsoever about the man's innocence, I should be the last
to want him freed.

The rest of the letter could best be described as the desperate pleas of a loyal wife who was trying her very best to save the life of the man she loved. For example, in relation to the fingerprints found at Evelyn Oatley's flat, she declares that 'In my humble opinion, neither of these prints belong to my husband'. Meanwhile, for the lies in her husband's statement concerning the time he signed back into his billet, her response was to say that the corporal on duty at the time did not report him for being late or for falsifying the time when he actually returned.

Marjorie claims that her husband had been let down by his barrister at the trial because he had failed to cross examine him after he had answered questions by the prosecution. She also says that the jury in the case had wrongly interpreted her husbands' lies over the booking in time at his billet as an attempt to create an alibi for the murder of Evelyn Oatley, saying that an unnamed airman who was being held at Feltham Prison could have been the murderer. She points out that another airman had tried to strangle a prostitute and although the police had been informed, the man in question had never been identified. Unfortunately, however, the letter was devoid of anything new for the Home Secretary to consider.

Documents #169 and #170 are from another two-page typed letter written by Cummins to his wife Marjorie, dated Wednesday, 10 June 1942.

My Darling,

I have not written until now, as for some reason I have been slightly depressed. I have, however, recovered my equanimity with the aid of your very welcome letter and Mary's cheerful scrawl.

Freda popped along to see me yesterday and was full of gossip. She mentioned a flat in Hampstead which may have been taken by now, I hope not.

It won't be long now. I await the appeal with trepidation. So much is at stake; do you think Pritt will be tired out by his present exertions on behalf of the Swindling person? I sound rather pessimistic, I know, but it's a natural reaction. I was too optimistic at the trial and got shaken a bit!

Friday

I gave this letter up as a bad job, some time ago, as you can see. The appeal is now lost, and all we have left is the faint hope of a reprieve. And as there is so much prejudice I doubt that it will come off. The governor has told me today that Der Tag [the day] *is Thursday, the 25ᵗʰ, and I have prepared myself for it. I am not afraid of death, but the manner of dying is just a little unusual and I feel the unmerited disgrace keenly. Also, it's a little disconcerting to know almost to the minute when the thing is coming off.*

I shall see you before you get this (that is if you come tomorrow), and I hope to hear of some progress in the matter of the reprieve. Kenwright has shown me the petition and I must say it is very well put. Unless Morrison is made of stone he must see the glaring discrepancies in the case against me, and must realise that it was improbable to bring them up at the trial or appeal. The law is an ass, isn't it?

Of course a long spell of penal servitude is a dreadful thing to look forward to, but I shouldn't think I'd be much more than forty on my release. That is, of course, if you are not successful in catching the actual guilty person. And it would have to be you, for the police would never admit a mistake even if they did catch him. It would cost them their jobs. I believe that reprieves, if and when they come, usually manage to turn up the night before the event, so don't lose hope even if we reach the last day without hearing anything. One thing is certain, Morrison has a tremendous responsibility; and even if the faintest doubt should assail him everything will be alright.

What sort of people are receiving father's statements? Sympathy and best wishes are useless if they don't write or pop along to see Morrison.

I know it's easy to talk, but, darling, if the worst happens I want you to carry on just as usual. You have your whole life in front of you, and it mustn't be wrecked just because your husband was an unlucky drunken fool. You may soon marry again, and find happiness with someone a bit more responsible than I. After all, I may only be beating fate to it by a short head. Flying isn't exactly safe in these times.

And you have the comfort of knowing that I am not the guilty person, not just because I am your husband, but after a careful study of all of the facts.

Our six years of married life have been happy; we have struggled together through difficult times, and each "hardship" has only served to increase my love for you. This present trouble has shown both me and the rest of the country that you are a wife in a million. Your courage and devotion will not pass unnoticed if there is a God.

My thoughts are centred on you day and night, darling, and if there is such a thing as life after death, then I shall always be by your side.

I am tired my dear, and I'm going to bed. Tomorrow cannot come quickly for me.

This awful silence breaks my heart,
This patience of the years.
The challenge of eternity
The tide of time and tears.
   G. A. Stoddart Kennedy.

Your adoring husband,
   GORDON

A very interesting letter indeed. One written by a condemned man having finally accepted his fate, whilst at the same time saying goodbye to his wife. He tells her to move on with her life, find happiness with another man, marry him and be happy. But perhaps what is most interesting about this letter is that despite the number of platitudes he pays her, he never once, in this particular letter, tells his wife that he loves her.

For most people finding themselves in such a situation, the words "I love you" would be one of the first things they would write in a letter. A psychopath, which I believe there is enough evidence to suggest Cummins was, cannot love a person in the way a normal person would. They are devoid of emotion, lack empathy and are self-absorbed individuals, but they can mimic love as a way of manipulating others. Psychopaths only enter into relationships for what the other person brings to it, thus fulfilling their own needs. Once they have what they want, they no longer have a need for the relationship. If Cummins was not a psychopath, how could he have so easily murdered four women in cold blood and then calmly returned to his billet as if nothing had happened?

Documents #180, #181 and #182 make up another letter Cummins sent to Marjorie from prison. Although it is not dated, it must have been written on 12 June as the prison governor advised the Home Secretary that Cummins had written to his wife in reply to her earlier letter to him.

Darling Marjorie,

Your letter came this morning and I have read it for perhaps the hundredth time. It is heartening to know that you believe in me. I am given confidence in the outcome of all this sordid business.

I do hope that D.N. Pritt has this case at his fingertips. Mr Kenwright seems to have confidence in him, but he also had

confidence in Flowers. If there is a failure, it will be a case of
"*Mors acerba, fama perpetua, stabit vetuo memoria facti.*"
[Death is bitter, but glory is eternal, the memory of my
deed will endure." Words uttered by Gerolamo Olgiati
whilst being tortured in 1476, after having been captured
for the murder of the Duke of Milan, Galeazzo Sforza.]

*I have made myself beautiful for a possible visit and jump
every time a key grates in the lock. So far nothing doing, but
there's still time. I sent the orders out yesterday. One each to
father, Mary, and the other* [to] *R.A.F. padre.*

*Dot's letter was short bit nice. Evidently she has not been
influenced by the* News of the World. *You must meet her,
and niece Sally, someday. Both of you have something in
common, erratic husbands, the source of many a headache.
Laurie was perhaps one of the most drunken fellows it was it
is possible to meet, due, I think, to the fact that he worked in
the bank. Also all members of his family are noted for their
eccentricity, less kind people would say madness, of course.*

*Our new flat. In which district are we to settle this time?
Hampstead or Curzon Street? Bermondsey or Whitechapel?
There is much to be said for Tooting Bec, and of course,
Wandsworth would be a good spot. It would serve as a
perpetual reminder and a strong deterrent.*

*Or perhaps the bridal suite at Keith Gibson's place, the
Spread Eagle would be more in our line? I could imagine
his leers coupled with the presentation of such a gift as we
received from him six years ago.*

*No visit yet, and its nearing tea time. I have a sort of
empty and lost feeling as though everyone has said, "Oh
to hell with him". I know that is not so, of course, the slips*

cannot have been received, so I must wait until tomorrow, and I'm used to waiting by now.

When I don't feel like reading or writing I play chess with one of the two officers who are always with me. Perhaps it is significant of my mental condition that I fail to see even the simplest of moves, leaving myself open to attack from all quarters. (In fact, on reflection, I think that has been characteristic of me all through this business.) I try to concentrate, with the unfortunate result that I only see vaguely some black and white pieces with absolutely no relation to one another.

By now I am convinced that there is no justice in this country. I, who am completely innocent, am sitting here waiting, and yet there was a certain man in Brixton with me on the same charge, murder. He admitted his guilt to us, and yet he was acquitted. There was also a few months ago a man who was found with a companion, in a house with a murdered woman. They were both dead drunk and their pockets were filled with her jewellery. One was acquitted and nulli casus brought against the other. Of course all these men were Canadian. Then there is the young Canadian soldier who shot two policemen. He was as sane as you or I, and he goes to Broadmoor, to work on a farm. Do you call that justice? A modern trial has developed into a lot of legal mumbo jumbo with a jury composed of self-opinionated grocers. Incidentally the jury system as first conceived was to have twelve men who <u>knew</u> both the plaintiff and defendant. These men were in a position to know small facts which might escape counsel.

But that's enough of that. The evil is done, and we must look forward, not back.

<u>Wednesday.</u>

I didn't feel I could write another word yesterday so I lost myself in a book, Hugh Walpoles "Roman Fountain". Once more I don my smart grey suit, my Moss Bros, and await the representatives of the outside world. Who will come, I wonder? Yours is the only visit that I await with eagerness, darling. I listen each morning and evening to the trains roaring by, and think to myself, "Marjorie might be on that".

I love you dearly, and I know that God (if there is one) cannot separate us much longer. I have been punished enough for my wayward habits, and I daren't think of the appeal, I come over all pessimistic.

See you on Saturday, honey.
Your adoring
Gordon

There is a noticeable difference in the tone of this letter to the one he previously sent to Marjorie on 2 May. Here, Cummins appears to be somewhat enveloped by melancholy. It is almost as if the seriousness of the situation has finally struck him, and for the first time he realises he is in real danger of losing his life. He appears full of self-pity, and his observations concerning other men he knows who have killed or carried out violent acts suggests he feels hard done by, or has been treated rather unfairly.

Cummins' father, John, sent a typed letter to the Home Secretary on 13 June, and is covered by documents #154, #155 and #156. As might be expected of a father in such circumstances, his loyalty towards his son was unwavering. His letter includes eighteen different points, each one challenging parts of the prosecution's case. His absolute belief of his son's innocence can clearly be seen in the letter's fourth paragraph:

> *These crimes are, collectively, the worst that have happened in recent times in this country and the perpetrator of them, whoever he is, should not be allowed to remain at large. He is evidently a sadistic, sexual maniac and should be treated as such, when found. My son has never shown any tendencies this way, and the fact that he has been happily married for six years, is known to be most patient, gentle and even-tempered, refutes any such idea.*

John Cummins mentions in his letter that his son did not receive a fair trial because although he only faced one count of murder, that of Evelyn Oakley, when the case came to court the allegations that Cummins was the man believed to be responsible for attacking the other women who had been murdered, had been widely reported in numerous national and local newspapers.

The unfairness was in two parts. Firstly, there could not have been many throughout the country who had not heard of, or read about, the story between the time of the murders and when the case finally came to court. This being so, John Cummins implies this therefore ensured his son did not receive a fair trial as the jury may already have made up their own minds.

Secondly, Cummins' legal team were informed by the prosecuting counsel, even as late as the night before the trial began, that if they called witnesses, of which there were many, to provide evidence of character in Cummins' favour, they would, in turn, vigorously attack him. As Cummins had no previous convictions, this could possibly mean that they would make reference to the attacks and murders of the other women and his suspected involvement. The problem for Cummins' counsel was that because they did not know specifically what evidence of "bad character" the prosecution intended to use, they could not provide any kind of defensive strategy to counter whatever allegations might come their way.

John Cummins refers to one report published in several newspapers, saying that Margaret Lowe's daughter had identified a cigarette case found on his son as belonging to her mother. Cummins senior claimed that what the daughter actually said was that it was "similar" to her mother's, and that the one discovered on his son had been given to him by his wife, Marjorie, some years previously.

The other valid question raised by John Cummins concerning his son's case was whether or not he had had a fair trial. There were no blood stains found on Cummins at the time of his arrest, or subsequently on any of his clothing, linking him to the murders of Oatley or any of the other three women. The jury which found Cummins guilty had been reading for weeks prior to the court case about the other women he was also alleged to have murdered and attacked, meaning that in essence they were judging him for the murders of all four women, as well as the attacks on the two who survived, and not just the murder of Evelyn Oatley. When it came to the appeal, Cummins' counsel, Mr D. N. Pritt KC, was hampered by only being allowed to include evidence and witnesses from the original case at the Old Bailey, when Cummins was convicted of the murder of Mrs Oatley. Evidence relating to the other three murders which, given its circumstantial aspects, may have painted a more favourable impression of Cummins, was not allowed to be presented at the appeal.

John Cummins wrote again to the Home Secretary on 24 June, the day before his son's execution; a final plea for a deferral whilst other evidence, which he believes his has unearthed, is investigated.

Sir,

I, the father of Frederick Gordon [sic] Cummins, make this final appeal to you to order a deferment of the execution of my son.

There is an accumulation of independent evidence now available to establish a prima facia case of miscarriage of justice.

By every rule of reason and justice no man should suffer death without the most careful investigation of every fact which may come to light before the moment of his execution.

The process of law is not infallible and although in the generality of cases there may be logical and conclusive proof of guilt, not displacement in the interim between sentence and execution, there are exceptions to this rule.

I take my oath that I am able to prove that all the facts relating to the murders in question have not been submitted to a jury, some of them because they were not known at the time of the trial, some because the prosecution then thought them irrelevant.

May I respectfully point out that the facts now known to me are also known to thousands of other loyal subjects of His Majesty and cause them the gravest concern and apprehension. If it should transpire that the haste of the law to execute a young man has deprived his father and his many friends of the chance to prove him innocent, there will be the most serious reflections on the administration of criminal justice in this country.

All I ask is that you, Sir, order the execution to be deferred until the evidence which I now have available has been carefully examined.

I realise that on the evidence already in your possession you are satisfied that guilt has been proved. But no evidence is conclusive so long as there is other evidence to refute that which has been available within a limited time.

If my son's life is taken by the law it cannot be put back, when later he is proved innocent. I submit, Sir, there can be no excuse for refusing to investigate new evidence, and I rest assured of your sense of responsibility in this matter.

I am, sir,
   Yours faithfully
   John R Cummins

As well as family members, Cummins also wrote, and presumably received, letters from friends. Document #280 is a letter dated 29 April 1942, written by Cummins to his good friend and colleague, Corporal Laurie Williams, a member of No. 600 Squadron, which at the time was stationed at RAF Predannack in Cornwall. The letter was also addressed to Williams' wife, Dot.

Dear Dot and Laurie,
   By this time you will, of course, have seen the news. The past few days have been a dreadful ordeal, and I am glad it is all over. Now that I am here, my father, our legal advisers

are, I hope, redoubling their efforts to find the guilty man, and prove my innocence before it is too late.

You will know of course that I was only tried on one case, obviously the one in which the prosecution thought they had the most evidence. Although John Flowers, my Counsel, put up a magnificent fight, it was no good. I am convicted on several so called "facts" which are ridiculous. (I hope I am not boring you). In the first place, parts of my original statement to the police are inaccurate, as to <u>time</u>, quite naturally, seeing that I was extremely drunk on the evening in question. To my horror the prosecution took the line, which was accepted by the judge, that the time errors were really an attempt to establish an alibi.

I was last seen on the evening in question by a woman at about 12.30, when I was making my way back to the billet. As of course there was no one who saw me after that, it is concluded that I murdered this woman then. There were in her flat, two fingerprints that Scotland Yard say are mine. Well, I don't know how they identify these things, but for every similarity, we could show at least two dissimilarities. These dissimilarities were brushed aside by Cherrill, the 'expert'. Those prints <u>cannot</u> have been mine, yet the jury accepted the police evidence.

Another 'fact' was that a cigarette case, without a doubt belonging to the woman, was found near my bedroom, four days after my arrest, although the police searched the place the day after my arrest. It was obviously planted by the guilty man.

When two of the murders happened (although it couldn't be mentioned at the trial) it was proved that I was in bed at the time, feeling unwell from the after effects of inoculation. There again articles belonging to the dead women were found near my room.

With all these facts in mind, and with the knowledge that the police were unable to find any blood stains on my clothing, my legal advisers were convinced of my innocence weeks ago, and they rightly thought that the culprit must be another cadet, and they started investigating. They found the man! There was, to their minds overwhelming proof of his guilt, so last week they laid their information before Scotland Yard. The police refused to act on it.

The facts we knew against this man did not consist of <u>proof</u>, so nothing could be said about it at the trial. However, now that I am sentenced to death I think my father is going to the Home Office to get things moving.

Incidentally, nothing could be said at the trial about my character which <u>might</u> have helped, because our dear friend Gwen had taken out a Summons against me. Thank her, will you?

<u>*Two Days Later.*</u>

My solicitor has just been to see me and I am appealing. Also he is hot on the trail of this other cadet.

Jerry seems to have made a mess of Bath, doesn't he? I wonder if the Christopher has been touched. Or the Hole in the Wall? Perhaps not, dens of iniquity nearly always escape unscathed! I'll bet Colerie was fog bound that night.

Give my regards to any of the lads who may still think well of me and of course Baillean, Dessy Farmer, John Owen, and

Nelson. Tell them that I'm eating well and being fattened up. Robinson or Morris never came to see me at Brixton; but I received a strange and illegible communication containing the Gospel according to St. John from "the boys" whoever they may be.

My love to Dot, and to niece Sally. If there's any justice in this world, I'll be seeing you all again. If not tell Gwen I'll come and haunt her.

I'll write again sometime and let you know how things are going on.

Yours optimistically
Gordon

The reference to "Gwen" in the letter could well be the owner of the Blue Peter Club in Falmouth, who Cummins sometimes helped out by working behind the bar. He had only been working there for a matter of weeks when she discovered he had been giving free drinks to some of his RAF colleagues. Soon after his dismissal, the same woman discovered that items of jewellery had been stolen from her apartment immediately above the Social Club. She reported the matter to the local police who, like her, suspected Cummins of the theft, but as there was no evidence to confirm their suspicions, the matter was not taken any further. It may have been just a coincidence that linked Cummins and the missing jewellery, but it does show that he may not have been as clean cut as previously thought.

Cummins wrote to Laurie and Dot Williams again in June, most likely in the week before his execution.

My Dear Dot and Laurie, not forgetting Sally,

I hardly know how to start this letter, as it is by way of being a sort of farewell note if there is no reprieve for me. As no doubt you know, the Great Day is next Thursday. My people, and Marjorie, are all working like the very devil to get a reprieve and bring the truth to light. We have a large backing, which includes the Archbishop of Canterbury, Sir Stafford Cripps, all the Quakers in the country, and a number of other prominent people. Father hopes to see the Home Secretary, and has already sent him eighteen sound and legal reasons why I shouldn't suffer the extreme penalty, in fact, I shouldn't be punished at all. All this is in addition to a sort of petition drawn up by D. N. Pritt, K.C., who knows the case inside out and who is convinced of my innocence.

The appeal failed because the only facts that can be used are those already used at the trial, and as there [sic] John Flowers badly mishandled the case, our hands were tied. Pritt fought magnificently, but we were up against the stone wall of subconscious prejudice. Most annoying.

You will read the mimeographed sheet that Marjorie sent you, and you can form your own opinions: it is only a <u>precis</u> of the tremendous evidence in my favour.

I have not had the pleasure and privilege of seeing the Press account of the trial and their description of my career, although I gather it was extremely libellous, in fact we have a libel action in hand against the Police as they were the only people who knew anything about my past life. However, you have read it and can judge the truth of the matter. For example, I have been described as a thief. As the only things

*I have ever pinched were some apples from an orchard at the
age of ten, the policeman who issued my life to the Press was,
to put it mildly, drawing the longbow.*

However, enough of that.

*Please give my very best wishes to those of my acquaintance
both inside the squadron and out. That includes Gwen and
more especially her mother, the Bosucton family, and the
Desenter. In the Squadron, don't forget Bill Baillean, and
Beatty. Tell Bill I am completely won over to his way of
thinking. "Topper", Dizzy Tramer, Bill Owen, Nelson and
Claringbull. Granny Rolfe (an honest man with the courage
of his convictions). Tell Nelson and Toppin that if they take
my advice they'll lay off booze and women. If not, be sure
to have plenty of witnesses at all times. Also would you say
what-ho to P/O Williams and say that in view of the flying
accident he and I had on Christmas day, it seems as though
Fate is determined to get me.*

*Let me know in time if the Squadron has done anything
worthwhile lately, accidents etc. And oh "Gosh", don't forget
Pat Wells and his wife Margaret "Gosh" Wells.*

*I've come to the awkward part of the letter. I find it very
difficult to put in to words exactly what I mean and feel.
I refer to the happy hours I have spent with Dot, you and
Sally. Sitting here in my cell, I have recalled these days,
and my heart is heavy. Rabbiting with that dreadful and
dangerous gun; the Cove, with old what's his name making
lobster pots, and wet days by the fire with Dot knitting like
hell. The evenings at the Blue Peter on either side of the
bar, Sally standing with her head against the wall. All these
things flash through my mind. For the moment I lose myself*

in thought, only to return to reality when a key grates in the door and someone comes in.

Give Sally a big kiss from me and there's a chaste one for you Dot. Keep Laurie on the straight and narrow, my dear. How's your finger Laurie? I purposely refrain from asking how it was done. Caught in some sort of trap, I suppose.

It's a pity you're so far away. I'd like to see you, nothing special to say, of course, but there you are.

No more old boy. I've bored you enough with this dreadful scrawl.

My love to you all,
GORDON

Laurie and Dot Williams were clearly good friends of Cummins, something which he does not appear to have had that many of, maybe suggesting that he was rather an acquired taste. While the letter is written with a certain calmness, it is hard to determine whether Cummins truly believed that the actions of his family and friends to stay his execution would eventually prove successful, or whether he was finally accepting of his fate.

The letters between Cummins, his family and acquaintances reveal three things. How much his wife, Marjorie, loved him, how they all believed his innocence without question, and just how utterly charming and convincing Cummins could be. The latter of these conclusions may well divide opinion.

Chapter Nine

The Murders of Maple Churchyard and Edith Humphries

As well as the murders committed in February 1942, Cummins is also suspected of previously carrying out two murders in October 1941, those of Maple Churchyard and Edith Humphries. Whilst researching and writing this book, I endeavoured to find out as much information about these two women as I could and was astonished to find that although information is held about both women at The National Archives (reference MEPO 3/2193), in both cases their "records" are closed. In the case of Edith Humphries, her file will not be opened until 1 January 2027, while Maple Churchyard's will not be opened until 1 January 2041. Why there is a disparity between the two dates, I do not know.

Unperturbed, on Saturday, 26 June 2021 I submitted a Freedom of Information request to The National Archives for the files of both women to be reviewed, with the intention of having them opened before their current due dates. On Monday, 28 June, less than forty-eight hours later, I received an e-mail from The National Archives to inform me that the record in question had been reviewed and the decision had been made to maintain its closed status. I was surprised to have received such an expedient reply, especially as The National Archives are closed to the public on Sundays and Mondays, although I fully appreciate that this does not necessarily mean their staff are not working behind the scenes. Even so, I still felt that this was an extremely quick reply given the circumstances. I was, and still am, not aware of the specific actions carried out when reviewing this case, but I did not feel that a detailed and thorough review of the record could have possibly been carried out in such a short period of time.

Below is a breakdown of the reply I received from The National Archives, informing me that a Freedom of Information assessor had reviewed the record and made the decision that its closed status would remain in place. After each section of the e-mail received, I have then included my comments and observations which formed part of my appeal against their decision not to open this record.

The first point they raised stated that changing the status of the record in question would prejudice Section 31 (1)(a)(b)(c) of the Freedom of Information Act 2000, which refers to the prevention and detection of crime, the apprehension or prosecution of offenders, and the administration of justice.

I pointed out that this was not relevant as the crimes in question, the murders of Maple Churchyard and Edith Humphries, had already taken place and had been officially designated as murders. I added that any potential suspects would have to be at least 100 years of age, and the chances of them still being alive were somewhat remote. I also added that I assumed as no arrests had taken place in the eighty years since the murders had occurred, there were consequently no active suspects.

They next addressed Section 38 (1)(a) of the Freedom of Information Act 2000, which is aimed at preventing an individual from having their physical or mental health endangered. Once again, I pointed out that as both victims were already dead, it was not possible for their physical or mental health to be endangered, making this argument irrelevant.

Part of the review process was a "public interest test", which was 'considered in consultation with the Metropolitan Police Service'. I asked what form the consultation with the Metropolitan Police took, and if there was a paper trail that evidenced this, adding that I believed whatever form this consultation had taken, it had been done so in an extremely quick period of time.

Next, under the heading 'Arguments made in favour of non-disclosure', came their justification for not opening the record:

> *This record contains information, which if released into the public domain would prejudice a future investigation/prosecution.*
>
> *It also contains information the disclosure of which would cause substantial mental anguish to the victim.*

I asked what specific information they were referring to. Was it a person's name, a street name, the name of a town, or a date? I also pointed out again that the two victims in this case were both dead, so it would not be possible for an early disclosure of the information to cause either of them any substantial mental anguish.

Regarding the matter of public interest, their statement said:

> *Exemption from disclosure of the information in this piece is sought because publication may prejudice a future investigation and prosecution. This case meets the criteria that indicates that it would be investigated in the future, if new evidence was adduced or a confession forthcoming:*
> * *This murder remains unsolved.*

- *The crime is of a seriousness that means it would merit further investigation.*
- *There is no age limit on the prosecution of persons suspected of murder.*
- *The suspect(s) may still be living.*
- *The record will document certain key evidence that could be used to identify alleged offenders or test the veracity of subsequent evidence / confessions.*

As has been previously pointed out, any suspect in this case, if still alive, would have to be at least 100 years of age. Point four in the above list mentions that the 'suspect(s) may still be living'. If there are known suspects in this case, who are they and are they still alive? Surely if the review of the Record in this case had been thoroughly carried out, it must be known if said suspect(s) were alive or dead?

The following was also included under the previous heading of public interest: 'This is a crime of such seriousness that even 50 years after the event the police would still pursue an investigation should the opportunity arise.' This is inaccurate as the crimes themselves took place in 1941, over eighty years ago, and is yet another example that shows how the Record was not thoroughly and comprehensively reviewed.

The email went on to state that: 'The premature release of this record into the public domain might, therefore, be detrimental to any future investigation and subsequent prosecution.' However, taking into account that both women are part of the same Record, why is the section on Edith Humphries closed until 1 January 2027, but that on Maple Churchyard closed until 1 January 2041? The difference between the two does not make sense. Using the same logic in The National Archives statement above, surely a disclosure in 2027 would be detrimental to any imminent investigation in regards to the killer(s) of Maple Churchyard? Next, the email states that:

> *This record also identifies several individuals who were victims of sexual assaults and attempted sexual assaults. Disclosure of this information would cause these individuals substantial mental anguish if disclosed into the public domain.*

The "several individuals" referred to here are clearly Evelyn Hamilton, Evelyn Oatley, Margaret Lowe and Doris Jouannet, the four women murdered by Cummins, along with Margaret Heywood and Catherine Mulcahy, who he attempted to murder. Each of their individual stories in relation to being one of Cummins' victims are well documented and have been for many years, so how 'disclosure of this information would cause these individuals substantial mental anguish if disclosed into the public domain', is unknown.

The e-mail ended with the following statement:

> *Information within the record is also covered by the exemption at section 40 (2) of the Freedom of Information Act. This exempts personal information about a 'third party' (someone other than the requester), if revealing it would break the terms of Data Protection Legislation. Data Protection Legislation prevents personal information from release if it would be unfair or at odds with the reason why it was collected, or where the subject had officially served notice that releasing it would cause them damage or distress. Personal information must be processed lawfully, fairly and in a transparent manner as set out by Art. 5 of the General Data Protection Regulation (GDPR).*

As both Maple Churchyard and Edith Humphries were both murdered in October 1941, they could not have served notice to any authoritative body that releasing information about them would cause either of them damage or distress as they were dead.

> *In this case the exemption applies because the record contains the personal and sensitive personal information of a number of identified individuals assumed still to be living. These individuals have a reasonable expectation of privacy which would not include the release of this information into the public domain by The National Archives during their lifetime. To do so would be likely to cause damage and/or distress and would be a breach of the first data protection principle, which is concerned with the fair, lawful and transparent processing of information of this kind.*

This final paragraph, I believe, shows just how poorly the review of this Record was conducted, because if a proper investigation of the case had been carried out, it would have seen that four of the individuals it was referring to had been murdered in February 1942.

That the relatives of Churchyard and Humphries are entitled to a reasonable expectation of privacy, and that the release of these files would cause them 'damage and/or distress', does not make sense. Although rules such as these are in place for sound reasons, which is understandable, they must still be balanced and include everybody and not just a few unnamed individuals. It is natural to think that most people with a relative who had been the victim of an unsolved murder would surely want to establish, to a degree of certainty, who had committed the crime, and would no doubt embrace and encourage any such investigation to discover the truth and unmask the individual(s) concerned.

In an attempt to justify why a record should remain closed, I do not believe it is fair, lawful or transparent to use the phrase 'identified individuals assumed still to be living'. The review should establish beyond all reasonable doubt whether the individuals referred to are in fact alive or dead, under Article 5 of the General Data Protection Regulation.

While I accept that I might be wrong in my assumption (and if I am, then I wholeheartedly apologise), but it appears to me that the answer I received for my request to have the Record concerning Maple Churchyard and Edith Humphries opened is a generic one, and that no actual investigation had been conducted. It is clear no effort was made to establish if the individuals referred to are still alive, or whether there are any known or outstanding suspects. Is there any physical evidence still in possession of the authorities from the murder of Maple Churchyard and Edith Humphries that has survived? If so, has it been tested in relation to try to establish a DNA profile?

To justify the reasons as to why a Record should or should not be opened, the answers provided must be relevant and exact. It cannot be right or proper to refer to an individual(s) as being 'assumed still to be living'. This needs to be clarified because if they are dead, then the reasons given for not opening a Record are, I would suggest, irrelevant. I have requested that a review be carried out of this decision and have provided detailed reasons as to why I felt this should be done. At the time of writing, no further response has been received.

On Friday, 23 July 2021, I received a further e-mail from a Freedom of Information Assessor, in response to my e-mail questioning their initial response to my request. Part of it read as follows: 'We have not yet decided if this record can be opened. We will respond to you by 05/08/2021. The National Archives has to consult other government departments in relation to this request.' There is no mention of which government departments the Assessor needed to consult with in relation to my request.

On 5 August, I received another e-mail from a Freedom of Information Assessor, which included the following statement: 'I am writing to inform you that we are required to conduct a public interest test in relation to your request and we will let you know the result of this by 02/09/2021.'

On 2 September, I received a further e-mail which included the following:

> *We wrote to you on 5th August 2021 to inform you that all of the information in this record is covered by a qualified exemption under the Freedom of Information Act 2000. This requires us to carry out a public interest test to determine whether the information can be released. The test is still being considered and we hope to have reached a decision by 29th September 2021.*

On 15 October 2021, I received yet another e-mail:

> *Dear Mr Stephen Wynn,*
>
> *Thank you for your enquiry of 27th June 2021 regarding a review of: MEPO 3/2195 – Murder of Edith Eleanora Humphries by person(s) unknown at Gloucester Crescent, NW1 on 17 October, 1941.*

Having considered the public interest test we have decided that this information should be withheld. I regret to say this means we cannot make this record open to you or to the public in general.

I previously explained that all of the information in the record is covered by sections 31 (1)(a)(b)(c) and 38 (1)(a) of the Freedom of Information Act 2000. Section 31 (1) exempts information if its disclosure under this Act would, prejudice (a) the prevention or detection of crime, (b) the apprehension or prosecution of offenders (c) the administration of justice.

Section 38 (1)(a) exempts information that, if it was released, would endanger the physical or mental health of any individual. A public interest test was considered in consultation with the Metropolitan Police Service. The outcome of which is as follows:

Arguments made in favour of disclosure

Disclosure of the information contained within this record would demonstrate how the police go about investigating serious crime.

The police service is accountable to the public it serves and it is in the common interest that information that demonstrates how it performs across the range of its duties is made available. However, this comes with the following caveats; such disclosures of information must not impede the police from discharging their lawful duties to detect and prevent crime, and identify, apprehend and bring offenders to justice; nor should disclosure infringe the rights of individuals.

Arguments made in favour of non-disclosure
This record contains information about the crime that, if released into the public domain, would compromise a future investigation and prosecution.

This record contains information that, if released into the public domain, would cause substantial anguish to the victim's surviving relatives.

Outcome of the public interest test
Exemption from disclosure of the information in this piece is sought because publication may prejudice a future investigation and prosecution. This case meets the criteria that indicates that it would be investigated in the future, if new evidence was adduced or a confession forthcoming.

This is a crime of such seriousness that even 77 years after the event the police would still pursue an investigation should the opportunity arise. Disclosure of the file into the public domain would risk sending the message that the police consider the case 'closed', which it is not, even after this period of time. The police would be failing in its duty to the public if it did not pursue a new line of enquiry even after this time, and therefore needs to ensure that its information is not compromised by inappropriate disclosure.

I responded by pointing out that the crime had actually been committed eighty years ago (to the very day) and not seventy-seven, as they had stated. I also highlighted that it is not the police who would make such a decision, but the Crown Prosecution Service.

In the next part of the email, the Assessor stated that:

> *It is not possible to identify particular information that might be released into the public domain without the risk of compromising any future police actions; information that appears innocuous may have significance to an experienced investigator that is not immediately obvious to the lay reader; or may assume a new significance in the light of newly discovered evidence or developments in forensic or investigative techniques. The evolution of new scientific techniques, especially the technology of DNA, means that cases hitherto considered unsolvable, are being examined afresh. Increasingly police services throughout the country are setting up 'cold case' teams to review their case files on unsolved murders; in some instances these unsolved murders date back to the 1940s.*

Is the murder of Edith Humphries currently a 'cold case' that is being reviewed by any police force across the United Kingdom? Is it likely to be treated as one any time soon?

The e-mail continued in a similar vein to the previous ones I had received on the matter, not really telling me anything new, or even answering any of the points which I had raised. It was like trying to get a politician to provide a yes or no to a straightforward question that they clearly did not want to answer.

> *The premature release of this record into the public domain might, therefore, be detrimental to any future investigation and subsequent prosecution.*

> *This record should remain closed citing s.31. This is*
> *because disclosure of the information contained therein could*
> *be prejudicial to a future investigation and prosecution with*
> *the result that a suspect may evade apprehension. Such an*
> *outcome would not be in the public interest.*
>
> *Additionally, this record contains information that graph-*
> *ically describes the trauma sustained by the victim in the*
> *form of crime scene and forensic reports and post-mortem*
> *and pathology reports. Disclosure of this information into*
> *the public domain would cause the surviving relatives*
> *substantial mental anguish.*

My response to this was that information is already in the public domain whereby the pathologist had stated Edith Humphries died from a stab wound to the head which pierced her brain, that her throat had been cut, and that she had also been strangled, although the latter was not the reason for her death. Despite these injuries, Edith Humphries did not die at the scene but in hospital. All this information is already available to the general public.

Regarding the surviving relatives of Edith Humphries, I pointed out that if the answer to this question was unknown, primarily because no such enquiries had been carried out, then surely that needed to be undertaken before such a reason that they would be caused 'substantial mental anguish' could be used.

Once again, rather than directly answering the question I had raised, the reply went into a previously quoted list of exemptions, sections and Acts and Data Protection Legislation, which they claimed prevented them from releasing the information I was requesting. One part of the answer appeared to be a complete contradiction of the very reasons they gave in not being able to provide the requested information in the first place.

> *Personal information must be processed lawfully, fairly and in a transparent manner as set out by Art. 5 of the General Data Protection Regulation (GDPR).*

Part of the email referred to the "subject" in the case, which in this instance was Edith Humphries. Having been murdered on 17 October 1941, she could not possibly have served notice that releasing personal information about herself would cause her damage or distress.

Once again, my efforts to ask them to release the files on Edith Humphries had simply fallen on deaf ears. Their replies continued to include the same phrases as to why they could not action my request to my satisfaction, such as 'sensitive personal material, reasonable expectation of privacy, breach of the first data protection principle,' as well as 'likely to cause damage and/or distress'.

The email closes by stating that the requester has the right to ask for an internal review if they are unhappy with the outcome, and that such requests must be submitted within two months of the date of the response.

I have, in fact, asked for an internal review as I was unhappy with the outcome, but this was to no avail. Yet again, my challenge was refused and the case files for Maple Churchyard and Edith Humphries will sadly remain closed until their original, respective, dates arrive.

Conclusion

Gordon Frederick Cummins was a murderer, of that there is no doubt. What is open to debate, however, is the exact number of women he killed. Although Cummins' lawyer suggested that items found at his billet, which linked him to the murders of Hamilton, Oatley, Lowe and Jouannet, were placed or planted there by somebody else, he provided no evidence to support this idea, making his comments nothing more than desperate words in an effort to deflect the attention away from his client.

Perhaps an even bigger question is why Cummins committed these murders? Was he deranged? Was he a sadistic sexual murderer? Or was he a psychopath? From research carried out during the writing of this book, I would suggest that he was the latter, although it must be pointed out that no medical practitioner had ever evaluated his mental capacity whilst he was alive, it is only subsequent to his death that attempts have been made to categorise him as such, based purely on his recorded behaviour.

When Cummins' actions are compared with those of the Yorkshire Ripper, Peter Sutcliffe, who murdered thirteen women and attempted to kill seven others between 1975 and 1981, it could be said that they were not too un-similar. But there has always been mixed debate surrounding Sutcliffe's claim to have heard voices from God telling him to kill prostitutes. There are those who say this was a fabricated claim simply so that he could be diagnosed with paranoid schizophrenia and sent to hospital, rather than a normal prison. There is, I believe, more credence to the claim that Sutcliffe's killing spree of prostitutes began because he was short-changed by one just a matter of weeks before killing his first known victim, Wilma McCann, on 30 October 1975. It is also rumoured that the same prostitute who short-changed him subsequently ridiculed him in a pub in front of others about the fact that he had a small penis. Not a claim most men would be happy about. However, I believe it was more the case that Sutcliffe was, in fact, a psychopath.

Both Sutcliffe and Cummins were married to women with whom they had perfectly normal relationships, and who they were never violent towards personally. The question in Cummins' case is what was it exactly that triggered his need and desire to murder and brutalise women he believed were prostitutes? There is no record, or suggestion, that Cummins suffered any kind of abuse in his youth. As is best known, he grew up in a loving family home with caring and attentive parents.

The most intriguing point is that he slit the throats of three of his victims after he had strangled them to the point of death, and certainly into a state of unconsciousness. When somebody is attacked and has their throat slit, this is an action which by its very nature is usually carried out from behind, as this would be the manner in which the perpetrator would grab hold of their intended victim. This has the added, but unintended, advantage of ensuring the attacker is not covered in blood spray from the wound caused to the victim's throat.

But why slit someone's throat after already having killed them by strangulation? There would be no need to do so from behind because the victim is already dead, which suggests that it may have been some kind of ritualistic blood-letting of the victim.

Why Cummins had such a need or desire to do this to his victims, women who he had never met before, or knew nothing about, is unclear. Maybe he had read a book about Jack the Ripper and was simply imitating what he had done. Sadly, we will never know the answer as he never took the stand at his trial or called upon any witnesses.

Thankfully, by leaving behind his gasmask and webbing belt, and keeping items belonging to his victims, Cummins provided the police with leads to track him down and evidence to prosecute and convict him with. In a day and age well before the technical advances society has today, it is anybody's guess as to how many more women Cummins could have murdered before he was caught. Or perhaps, like his predecessor Jack the Ripper, his identity may never have been discovered.

No story about Cummins can be complete, though, without looking at the question of whether or not he received a fair trial. Before his case reached the Old Bailey, news of the murders of the four women had been comprehensively reported in both regional and national newspapers for weeks. Cummins was not only named as being the main suspect, but it was reported that he had also been charged with all four murders. The chances of the majority of the British public having not heard of the murders, and Cummins' link to them, are slim at best.

The members of the jury at his Old Bailey trial only had to make a decision as to whether or not they believed he had murdered Evelyn Oatley, because it was only her murder he was on trial for. Yet the reality was that they were more than likely also thinking about the murders of Evelyn Hamilton, Margaret Lowe and Doris Jouannet. How could they have not been when they had been reading about them, and how Cummins had been originally charged with their murders, for weeks? The same could be said about his appeal. How could the judges not have heard or read about his connection to all four murders?

The other aspect which comes into the discussion of whether Cummins received a fair trial was the decision to only charge him with the murder of Evelyn Oatley. Maybe that was simply a ploy by the prosecution to secure a conviction, because hers was the only one where the defence could not put forward a strong enough alibi.

Imagine, if you will, Cummins standing trial for the murders of all four women, where his defence team were able to put forward strong and plausible arguments that were enough to cause doubt in the minds of the jury, and that he had not been responsible for just one of the murders, but all four. The ambiguity and insufficient evidence might just have been powerful enough to sway them in to having found him not guilty. It most certainly could have made a big enough difference at his appeal to have saved him from the gallows.

Sources

www.nationalarchive.org

www.cwgc.org

www.ancestry.co.uk

www.britishnewspaperarchives.co.uk

www.psychologytoday.com

1911 Census for England and Wales

1939 England and Wales Register

www.in2013dollars.com

www.unsolved-murders.co.uk

1939 England and Wales Register

UK Burial and Cremation index, 1576–2014

www.psychopathsinlife.com

www.mindhuntersinc.com

About the Author

Stephen is a happily retired police officer having served with Essex Police as a constable for thirty years between 1983 and 2013. He is married to Tanya, who is also his best friend.

Both his sons, Luke and Ross, were members of the armed forces, collectively serving five tours of Afghanistan between 2008 and 2013. Both were injured on their first tour. This led to Stephen's first book *Two Sons in a Warzone – Afghanistan: The True Story of a Fathers Conflict*, which was published in October 2010.

Both of Stephen's grandfathers served in and survived the First World War, one with the Royal Irish Rifles, the other in the Mercantile Navy, whilst his father was a member of the Royal Army Ordinance Corp during and after the Second World War.

Stephen corroborated with one of his writing partners, Ken Porter, on a previous book published in August 2012, *German POW Camp 266 – Langdon Hills*. It spent six weeks as the number one best-selling book in Waterstones, Basildon between March and April 2013. They have also collaborated on four books in the 'Towns & Cities in the Great War' series by Pen and Sword. Stephen has also written other titles for the same series of books and in February 2017 his book, *The Surrender of Singapore: Three Years of Hell 1942-45*, was published. This was followed in March 2018 by *Against All Odds: Walter Tull, the Black Lieutenant*. October 2018 saw the publication of *Animals in the Great War* and in January 2019, *A History of the Royal Hospital Chelsea – 1682-2017: The Warriors' Repose*, both written with his wife, Tanya.

March 2019 saw the publication of his book *Disaster before D-Day: Unravelling the Tragedy of Slapton Sands*. In March 2020, his book *Mystery of Missing Flight F-BELV*, was published, focussing on the personal story of the death of his uncle during the Vietnam War. The same month saw the publication of *City of London at War: 1939-45*. April 2020 saw the publication of *Holocaust: The Nazis' Wartime Jewish Atrocities, and* in June 2020, his book *Churchill's Flawed Decisions: Errors in Office of the Greatest Britain*, was published.

Stephen has co-written three crime thrillers which were published between 2010 and 2012, and centre round a fictional detective named Terry Danvers.

When he is not writing, Stephen and Tanya enjoy the simplicity of going out for a morning coffee, lunch time meals or walking their four German shepherd dogs early each morning, whilst most sensible people are still fast asleep in their beds.

Index